PRAGMATICS

Pragmatics: The Basics is an accessible and engaging introduction to the study of verbal and nonverbal communication in context.

Including nine chapters on the history of pragmatics, current theories, the application of pragmatics, and possible future developments in the field, this book:

- Offers a comprehensive overview of key ideas in contemporary pragmatics and how these have developed from and beyond the pioneering work of the philosopher Paul Grice;
- Draws on real-world examples such as political campaign posters and song lyrics to demonstrate how we convey and understand direct and indirect meanings;
- Explains the effects of verbal, nonverbal, and multimodal communication and how the same words or behaviours can mean different things in different contexts, including what makes utterances more or less polite;
- Highlights key terms and concepts throughout and provides chapter-end study questions, further reading suggestions, and a glossary.

Written by an experienced researcher and teacher, this book will be an essential introduction to this topic for all beginning students of English language and linguistics.

Billy Clark is Professor of English Language and Linguistics at Northumbria University, UK.

The Basics

The Basics is a highly successful series of accessible guidebooks which provide an overview of the fundamental principles of a subject area in a jargon-free and undaunting format.

Intended for students approaching a subject for the first time, the books both introduce the essentials of a subject and provide an ideal springboard for further study. With over 50 titles spanning subjects from artificial intelligence (AI) to women's studies, *The Basics* are an ideal starting point for students seeking to understand a subject area.

Each text comes with recommendations for further study and gradually introduces the complexities and nuances within a subject.

For a full list of titles in this series, please visit www.routledge.com/The-Basics/book-series/B

PRAGMATICS

THE BASICS

Billy Clark

Routledge
Taylor & Francis Group

LONDON AND NEW YORK

First published 2022
by Routledge
2 Park Square, Milton Park, Abingdon, Oxon OX14 4RN

and by Routledge
605 Third Avenue, New York, NY 10158

Routledge is an imprint of the Taylor & Francis Group, an informa business

British Library Cataloguing-in-Publication Data
A catalogue record for this book is available from the British Library

Library of Congress Cataloging-in-Publication Data
Names: Clark, Billy, author.
Title: Pragmatics: the basics/Billy Clark.
Description: London; New York: Routledge, 2021. | Includes bibliographical references and index. |
Identifiers: LCCN 2021007125 (print) | LCCN 2021007126 (ebook) |
Subjects: LCSH: Pragmatics.
Classification: LCC P99.4.P72 C53 2021 (print) | LCC P99.4.P72 (ebook) | DDC 401/.45–dc23
LC record available at https://lccn.loc.gov/2021007125
LC ebook record available at https://lccn.loc.gov/2021007126

ISBN: 978-1-138-19385-7 (hbk)
ISBN: 978-1-138-19386-4 (pbk)
ISBN: 978-1-003-19726-3 (ebk)

Typeset in Bembo
by Deanta Global Publishing Services, Chennai, India

For Ohna, Apoa, Kiloh, and wonananoland.

CONTENTS

LIST OF FIGURES AND TABLES

FIGURES

TABLE

ACKNOWLEDGMENTS

I am as grateful as can be to the students, teachers, family, and friends I have learned with over the years, in a wide range of interactions and contexts, in classrooms, corridors, coffee shops, conferences, in reading, writing, and other media.

There are too many names to mention here but the teachers I am most grateful to include Spence Rae, Gert Ronberg, Graham Trengove, Ruth Kempson, Neil Smith, Dick Hudson, Deirdre Wilson, and Robyn Carston. I have learned from many students and colleagues and can only mention a tiny number of them here. Thank you to Aisha Abugharsa, Salwa El-Awa, Maitrayee Basu, Salim Bouherar, Patricia Canning, Anna Charalambidou, Cris Chatterjee, Paul Cobley, Ilse Depraetere, Alan Durant, Alex Golding, David Keeble, Benoît Leclercq, Kyu Hyun Park, Ramona Pistol, Kate Scott, Sylvia Shaw, Hanna Stöver, Naoko Togame, Tim Wharton, and Mai Zaki. The groups too large to pick names from are, of course, the students in schools, undergraduate and taught postgraduate programmes, who have had the most profound influence on my understanding of pragmatics and other topics over many years.

I am grateful to Brian Walker, Kate Scott, Kiloh Falby Clark, Robert McKenzie, and Siobhan Chapman for very helpful comments on a draft version of the book, and to Lan Hoang Thy Anh for help with the Vietnamese examples.

I am very grateful to Lizzie Cox, Adam Woods, Nadia Seemungal Owen, and all at Routledge for support and patience through the long period in which the book was produced.

Finally, I owe a special debt to Kate Scott for encouraging me to keep this project going and to Dotori on Stroud Green Road for sustenance in the very strange contexts of 2020.

CONVENTIONS

There are only a few conventions which I have needed to use in the book. I have tried to keep technical terms to a minimum but, as with most research areas, some of these are unavoidable. There are brief definitions for technical terms in the glossary near the end of the book. Here are brief explanations of typographical conventions and of how I have represented sounds.

TYPOGRAPHICAL CONVENTIONS

Linguistic expressions:
When I refer to a linguistic expression I write it in italics, e.g. when discussing words such as *morning* and *coffee* or the phrase *a morning coffee*

Concepts:
These are represented in small caps and sometimes with curly brackets around them, e.g. if I talk about the concept {COFFEE} I will sometimes write COFFEE and sometimes {COFFEE}

Interpretations and meanings in contexts:
When I discuss what an utterance conveys or how it is understood I have written this either in standard orthography (i.e. like these words) or in inverted commas. So I might say that an utterance of the expression *coffee* on a particular occasion is intended to represent the 'hot

drink' sense of coffee or that it communicates that the speaker is offering the hearer coffee.

SOUNDS

When I needed to represent sounds, I have used symbols from the International Phonetic Alphabet (IPA), produced and updated by the International Phonetics Association (https://www.internationalphoneticassociation.org). I hope that I always make clear enough what sound each symbol is intended to represent. You can find the IPA charts here:

https://www.internationalphoneticassociation.org/content/ipa-chart

When transcribing sounds for a particular variety, there is always some idealisation involved, and the transcriber has to make decisions about how to represent particular sounds. I have not discussed this much here but of course there are lots of useful textbooks and other resources where you can find out more.

If you would like to type IPA symbols yourself, there is a useful tool here:

https://ipa.typeit.org

If you'd like to find out more about what your body is doing when you make individual sounds, this site is very useful:

https://seeingspeech.ac.uk

It includes videos of sounds which you can view by clicking on IPA symbols here:

https://seeingspeech.ac.uk/ipa-charts/

PROSODY

I have assumed a fairly simple set of tones for English here, as follows:

Fall:	\	Rise:	/
Rise-Fall:	∧	Fall-Rise:	∨
Level:	—		

PREFACE

This book is about 'the basics' of pragmatics, which is about how we communicate and understand each other in various kinds of interaction. A very wide range of topics falls within the scope of work in pragmatics so the book can only cover the basics of part of this. I focus mainly on pragmatics as the study of inferences involved in communication developing from the work of the twentieth-century philosopher Paul Grice. I also focus mainly on the pragmatics of varieties of English. Interactions are, of course, affected by cultural and linguistic contexts so the ideas discussed here will apply differently in different cultural and linguistic contexts. The book aims to give you a sense of the basics so you can then move on to consider more complex questions, including about how things vary around the world.

A starting point for work in pragmatics is the observation (made at least as long ago as ancient Greece) that the same words used on two different occasions can mean different things. We can refer to almost any linguistic expression to illustrate this. Words like *here* and *now* change their meaning depending on who says them when. Words like *yes*, *yeh*, or *aye* can indicate agreement with something not explicitly expressed and we need to know something about who said it when to know what is being agreed with. These expressions can also be used for other purposes, e.g. we might cry out '*Yes!*' when something good happens (for example, if our football team has scored a goal or we have been offered a job we really want).

The word *basic* itself also has meanings other than the one intended in the title of this book and book series. Currently, at least in parts of the UK and the United States, it can be used negatively to indicate that somebody is predictable, unimaginative, uninspiring, etc. Like many words, the exact meaning of the term varies, with different people understanding it differently and the same person using it differently in different contexts. The online Cambridge English Dictionary currently lists this meaning:

boring and not unusual or surprising in any way
(https://dictionary.cambridge.org/dictionary/english/basic   accessed
    4 January 2021)

While I was working on this book, my daughter bought me a can of beer whose name refers playfully to this sense. It's called 'Am I Being Basic?' You can see the label on the can here: https://pressuredrop brewing.co.uk/blogs/beers/am-i-being-basic-6-8-neipa

The changes in the meaning of *basic* are about linguistic semantics. The word has been developing a new linguistic meaning alongside earlier ones. Pragmatics focuses on how we work out which meaning is intended when words are uttered in a specific situation.

The word *pragmatics* is also understood differently by different researchers. It can be used very broadly to include almost any topic connected with interaction. In the sense I focus on in this book, it is about how we communicate and understand each other. It aims to develop accounts of how we decide which words to use, and what other things to do, while communicating, about how we work out what someone intends to communicate by what they say and do, and about how meanings emerge and are adjusted during interaction. I hope to convince you that pragmatics is fascinating and important, that it is central to understanding language and communication, and that ideas from pragmatics are relevant and useful in a wide range of contexts, including everyday interactions and various types of professional and mediated communication.

Pragmatics has developed considerably in recent decades. The book aims to give you an idea of where pragmatics is at the moment, how it got there, and how it might develop in future. It begins with an indication of what pragmatics is and what kinds of questions it should aim to answer (some of which are closer to being answered than others). It then considers the work of the philosopher Paul Grice and approaches which have developed from his initial ideas. It considers some of the further complexities of interaction, some of the ways in which ideas have been tested and applied, and it considers where pragmatics might go in the future.

There are some very complicated ideas in pragmatics but the 'basics' are not hard to grasp and I hope the discussion here is easy to follow. Each chapter ends with brief suggestions for things to do to find out more, including some suggested further reading. There is a fuller bibliography, including some online resources, at the end of the book.

I hope you find the book useful and that it inspires you to go beyond the basic ideas presented here.

INTRODUCTION
THE VERY BASICS

This chapter discusses what pragmatics is and what it aims to explain. The term 'pragmatics' has been used in many ways and to cover a very wide range of things. This book focuses on pragmatics understood as being about how we work out (or '**infer**') what to say, write, sign (in sign languages), and do when communicating, and how we work out ('infer') what others are intending to communicate to us. The chapter looks at some things (not everything) which pragmatic theories have attempted to explain. We begin to consider possible explanations in Chapter 2.

COMMUNICATING AND UNDERSTANDING

Have you ever misunderstood something? Or been misunderstood? Have you ever wondered why some interactions make you feel happy or frustrated? Maybe you notice that you always feel good after you've had a conversation with one friend and not so good after you've spoken to another? Or maybe that you sometimes annoy or offend somebody without meaning to? Have you ever noticed that some people have a knack for getting what they want from other people in everyday interactions or in workplace contexts? Or that things often go wrong for somebody else? Understanding these things usually involves some consideration of pragmatics. This is because pragmatics is about what we do when we communicate and how we respond to other people's communicative acts.

There are many approaches to pragmatics, and they focus on a very wide range of topics. Pragmatics as understood in this book aims to account for how we produce and understand acts of verbal and nonverbal communication. Most current work on pragmatics developed from work on language which focused initially on how contextual factors affect the interpretation of linguistic utterances. In particular, the focus was on how we work out or 'infer' meanings in specific contexts. Later work broadened the discussion to consider a wider range of aspects of verbal and non-verbal communication and to production and interaction as well as interpretation.

We infer, or 'make inferences', all the time. I made several today. I saw bright light in the window and inferred that it was a sunny day. I heard the letterbox open and close and inferred that the post had arrived. I saw a flattened empty cereal packet and inferred that the cereal was finished. And I made many more inferences as I went about my day.

We also make inferences when communicating. Here is an example to illustrate this (the part in italics represents some contextual information):

(1) *A man (Adam) walks into a room where a TV is switched on. He picks up the remote and turns the TV off. He then turns around and sees a woman (Bella) sitting in an armchair.*
Bella: I was watching that!

What happens next? A reasonable guess is that Adam might turn the TV on again and (probably) apologise, maybe also saying something intended as an explanation (e.g. 'Sorry, I didn't see you.')

How do we explain what happened in (1)? At first glance, this probably seems straightforward. Bella is upset that Adam turned the TV off and makes this clear by pointing out that she was watching it.

However, what I have just written does not explain things. It just describes them using different words. An explanation would need to tell us more about what both Adam and Bella did, including how they decided what to do and say, and how they each understood what the other had said and done. A full account of what happened would involve a large number of things, including accounts of:

(2) a.   what Adam thought (and inferred) when he entered the room
   b.   how Adam decided to turn off the TV
   c.   what Bella thought when Adam turned the TV off
   d.   how Bella decided what to say
   e.   how Adam worked out what Bella intended

If we stayed in the room, we'd have more to consider, including how Adam decides what to do next (e.g. realising his mistake and offering an explanation), and so on.

Pragmatics usually focuses on the last of these, i.e. on (2e). More specifically, it usually focuses on how Adam got from the linguistic meaning of what Bella said to an understanding of what she intended in this context, i.e. on how Bella's utterance led Adam to work out that Bella was saying (directly) that she was watching the TV programme and (indirectly) that she was upset that Adam had turned it off and that she would like it turned back on again. When we list what we need to explain, it's quite a long list. We might summarise by saying that it aims to explain how Adam recognises the following things (among others):

(3) Understanding *I was watching that*:
   a.   linguistic form
      I was watching that
   b.   linguistic meaning
      The person referred to as *I* was watching the thing referred to as *that* at some point before the time when she said it
   c.   contextual assumptions
      Bella is the speaker
      Adam has turned off the TV in the room he just came into
      Bella was sitting opposite the TV Adam turned off
   d.   directly communicates
      Bella was watching the programme which was showing on the TV which Adam has just turned off
   e.   indirectly communicates
      Bella is not happy about what Adam has done
      Bella would like the TV turned on again

An account of how utterances are understood in this way has been at the core of pragmatics since it took off as an area of study in the mid to late twentieth century.

More recently, there has been increased focus on how we decide what to say or do when we produce communicative acts as well as on how we interpret them. There has also been increased interest in the notion that what is communicated involves communicators working together to 'co-create' or 'negotiate' what is communicated. On this view, the overall meaning of this interaction is constructed by Adam and Bella working together rather than just Adam thinking about what Bella has (done and) said. This also involves not simply treating each turn in an interaction separately but instead considering how communication extends across all of the interactive behaviour and, for some approaches, beyond this.

We will see also that pragmatics now also focuses on other things, including on nonverbal communication and on 'prosody', which is about the way utterances sound or are signed when they're produced, including pitch movements, rhythm, pace, volume, voice quality, duration of signs, use of signing space, and so on. In this example, Bella might, for example, produce an utterance which gets louder and more high-pitched towards the end. Or she might say it in a more monotone way. There are lots of possibilities, and these would affect how Adam understands her. There are also things Bella might have done other than speaking which affect Adam's understanding, e.g. raising her eyebrows, opening her eyes wide, or raising her hands outwards to her side.

The rest of this book considers some of the ways in which pragmatic theorists have tried to explain how we communicate and understand each other, including in nonverbal as well as verbal communication. This rest of this chapter considers a number of questions (not all) about Bella's utterance and the wider interaction which we might expect pragmatic theories to provide answers for. We might evaluate pragmatic theories by considering to what extent they provide answers to each of these.

WHAT PRAGMATICS AIMS TO EXPLAIN

Pragmatics can be understood as being about things which are communicated beyond the meanings of linguistic expressions used. Early work focused mainly on what's communicated indirectly (e.g.

that Bella is upset with Adam in the example we just discussed). There is more to explain than this, including how we work out what is directly communicated (that Bella was watching the TV in this example). Later work has recognised that we need to make inferences to work this out as well. Most theorists also now assume that pragmatics should say something about what communicators do. This section mentions some but not all of the things which pragmatic theories should aim to explain.

WHAT IS BELLA COMMUNICATING DIRECTLY?

Adam needs to work out what Bella is communicating directly by her utterance, i.e. what exactly the words *I was watching that* 'mean' here. More technically, we might say that Adam needs to work out what proposition Bella is representing here. Roughly, this means what statement her utterance represents. In semantics and pragmatics, a proposition is something that can be evaluated to see whether it's true or false. It might seem obvious what proposition Bella is expressing here, partly because we have some idea of the context in which she said it. Imagine, though, that somebody asked you whether '*I was watching that*' is true right now without letting you know who said it when, where, and who they were talking to. You wouldn't be able to answer until you knew at least who the word *I* referred to and what the word *that* referred to. In fact, you'd also need to know something about the time or circumstances in which the watching took place. Here are rough characterisations of some things it could mean in different contexts:

(4) a. Bella was watching the TV Adam turned off at the time when he pressed the off button.
   b. Calum was watching the 2020 Emmy Awards ceremony when Zendaya won the award for Outstanding Lead Actress in a Drama Series.
   c. Dani was watching the TV series *Euphoria* when it was first broadcast in 2019.
   d. Ed was watching when his daughter sneaked a chip from her brother's plate while they were eating together.

In order to work out what is directly communicated, we need at least to work out what is being referred to by any of the referring expressions (including personal pronouns like *I* and demonstrative pronouns like *that*) and decide at what time or situation the event referred to is seen as taking place. Referring expressions also include proper names like *Adam*, *Bella*, *Calum*, *Dani*, and *Ed*. (In fact, we haven't identified clear referents above as we've only used the names themselves which means they could refer to anybody referred to by that name.) Other referring expressions include noun phrases such as *the student with the blue rucksack* (these are called definite descriptions as they identify an individual) and *a student with a spare copy of the textbook* (indefinite descriptions as we cannot uniquely identify an individual referent for them).

We can think of working out the time or circumstances in which events take place as another kind of reference assignment and one which we always need to work out. It's important to notice that the past tense does not only indicate that the event happened before the time of the utterance. In (4a), the time is one which starts before Bella's utterance (we and Adam do not know how far back the watching began) and continues until when Adam pressed the button. In (4b), the time is further back and covers an indeterminate amount of time when the winner of the award was announced. In (4c), we understand that Dani watched episodes of *Euphoria* either one at a time or in larger chunks around the time when they were first available. In (4d), we understand that Ed was watching the key moment at the table when his daughter took a chip from her brother's plate. An important thing to notice here is that we do not need to be certain of exactly what time or situation is being referred to in order to think that we have an understanding of the utterance.

It might not be clear here why we say 'time or circumstances' rather than simply 'time' when thinking about when events occur. This is because there are cases where the time is not important but the situation is, as here:

(5) Whenever I ask Adam to do something with me, he's always busy.

In both clauses here, there is not a specific time in mind but any situation in which the speaker asks Adam to do something.

There are other kinds of things we need to work out in order to understand what somebody has said directly. I'll mention three of them here: disambiguation of ambiguous expressions, working out what has been left out in elliptical ('missed out') expressions, and what is sometimes called 'free enrichment' where no linguistic material is thought of as missing but we still work out a bit more.

DISAMBIGUATION

In linguistics, the term ambiguous usually has a narrower definition than in everyday conversations. In everyday contexts, we can say that somebody is being ambiguous whenever it is not clear exactly what they intend. In linguistics, the term is usually reserved for cases where a linguistic expression is associated with more than one linguistic meaning.

One kind of ambiguity is termed 'lexical ambiguity'. This is where a word has more than one possible meaning. There are lots of examples in all languages. In British English, the word *boot* can refer, among other things, to an item of footwear or to the space at the back of a car for storing things. We can see that ambiguity depends on what language you speak by considering other languages. In French, for example, the two senses of *boot* are not associated with the same word. The most common word for the 'footwear' sense is *botte*. For the part of a car, the most common word is *coffre*. In US English, *boot* is used for the footwear sense but the other sense would usually be referred to with the word *trunk* (also ambiguous as it can refer to an elephant's nose, a large item of luggage or storage, and other things).

Lexical ambiguity arises for various reasons, often because of language change. Sometimes this involves a coincidence, e.g. the fact that *match* can mean a small wooden thing for starting a fire or a person or thing that is in some sense similar or equal to another has come about through historical accident. Strictly speaking, linguists would usually say that there are (at least) two words *match* which have different senses (rather than one word with more than one sense). In other cases, new words emerge which are related to earlier senses, e.g. *mouth* as in part of a human face or the place where a river meets the sea, where the latter has emerged from metaphorical uses of the former. The term 'polysemy' is often used to refer to cases where a word has distinct senses which are seen as connected to some extent but it is not always clear what counts as close enough to describe a word as polysemous.

In fact, some theorists suggest that word meanings are adjusted every time they are used in order to understand exactly what a speaker intends. If I am standing by a whiteboard, for example, and ask if you have a 'pen', you are not likely to offer me a biro but you might offer me a whiteboard marker if you have one. We might understand this as a case where the intended meaning is narrower than the more general standard meaning. Other cases can be understood as involving 'looser' than standard meanings. I might, for example, describe the venue for a concert as 'empty' even though a few people were in the audience. Here is a real example from a website where a band member describes 'playing to empty venues' and suggests that this can be a positive:

(6) And it sucked playing to an empty hall after all that big build up, on the plus side the massive amount of drinks and having just 4 peeps in the audience made us less nervous. From: https://rockbandsinlondon.wordpress.com/2011/07 /21/performing-to-empty-rooms/

This is just one of several examples in the article where it is clear that 'empty' really means 'close to empty' as there are some 'peeps' (people) in the audience.

When words are used fairly often with similar adjusted meanings, this can lead to us deciding that the word has developed a new meaning. When we describe water we have been swimming in as 'boiling' or 'freezing' nowadays, our addressees are unlikely to think that the 'boiling' water is really at 100 degrees centigrade or that the 'freezing' water is really so cold that it is solid. We might say that these words are polysemous as they can have their original technical sense in some contexts. A much-discussed example of a loosening which has become established concerns the word *literally* which is now often used with a sense that was originally non-literal. A typical usage might be if someone says that one football team 'literally destroyed' another in a match. Similarly, a colleague of mine once told me that they had received 'literally millions' of emails about a particular topic. There is some complexity here as we could argue that *literally* is retaining its meaning but that the words around it are not being used literally. The fact that the original meaning still exists is, of course, part of the explanation for why some people object to the 'less than literal' sense.

Structural ambiguity (also known as 'syntactic ambiguity') occurs when a linguistic expression has more than one meaning due to the possibility of assigning two different structures to it. One kind of example occurs with conjunctions such as *learner drivers and motorcyclists* in this example:

> (7) We shouldn't allow learner drivers and motorcyclists on the new bypass.

On one reading the speaker or writer means that learner drivers and learner motorcyclists should not be allowed. On another reading, the aim would be to ban learner drivers and all motorcyclists.

It is easy to miss structural ambiguities. Here is an example from a newspaper article about Italian food which the writer (Rachel Roddy) clearly neither noticed nor intended:

> (8) Earlier this summer, I spent a day cooking with a young chef called Alessandro Venturi, who is originally from Rome and is now making and serving some of the best Roman food you will eat from a food truck in York.
> Rachel Roddy. Tales from an Italian kitchen. The Guardian, 26 September 2020.
> https://www.theguardian.com/food/2020/sep/28/rachel-roddy-recipe-for-pasta-with-sausage-leek-and-mascarpone

I assume that this means that Venturi serves 'some of the best Roman food you will eat' and that it is served 'from a food truck in York' rather than that of all 'the Roman food you will eat from a food truck in York', this is some of the best. It's easy to spot examples of structural ambiguity if, for example, you can spot noun phrases with more than one modifier before the main noun. I just heard the film critic Mark Kermode say he is a '*huge disaster movie fan*'. Have a think about what the options are here, e.g. is he a fan of movies that are huge disasters? Or is he a disaster movie fan who is also huge? (This reading involves a bit of lexical ambiguity too, of course).

ELLIPSIS

Ellipsis is the term for cases where we understand that speakers have not pronounced some linguistic material which they could have said, trusting hearers to work out what is missing. Here are two examples:

(9)   Adam: Calum needs a model to practise on for his hair-
dressing exam. Can you do that for him?

Bella: I don't want to.

(10)   Adam: Bella says she'll help Calum with his homework if
Calum helps with hers.

Dani: Seems reasonable.

In (9), we can see that Bella means that she doesn't want to be a model
for Calum and has assumed that we will know what it is that she doesn't
want to (do). In (10), Dani has missed out the subject and trusted Adam
to work out that she (Dani) thinks that what Bella has proposed seems
reasonable. There are many cases in everyday conversation and in other
contexts where we 'miss out' some linguistic material like this and
assume that our addressees will work out what we mean.

OTHER ASSUMPTIONS

There are other things we assume when working out what somebody
has directly communicated. Here are three examples:

(11)   I'm ready.

(12)   The temperature's dropped.

(13)   Bella's got skills.

We are not likely to assume that the speaker of (11) is just ready for
something or other. Instead, we will decide that she is ready for something in particular, e.g. that she is ready to go for a walk or to have
a discussion about something. In (12), we will make an assumption
about where the temperature has dropped and/or what has undergone
a change in temperature, e.g. the outside temperature in our location
(due a change in the weather), or the temperature in the room we are
in. We might also assume that the temperature of a particular thing has
dropped, e.g. of an oven or a fridge. In (13), we are likely to make an
assumption about the kinds of skills Bella has, e.g. as a skateboarder or as
a cook. Exactly what we decide in each case will depend on the context.

WHAT IS BELLA COMMUNICATING INDIRECTLY?

When you read 'I was watching that' in the example above, I am
sure that you assumed more than what you think Bella communicated

directly, i.e. that Bella had been watching the TV that Adam turned off. You are very likely also to have assumed that she was trying to communicate something indirectly. Here are some things you might have assumed that Bella intended:

(14) a. Bella is unhappy that Adam turned the TV off
     b. Bella wanted to carry on watching the TV
     c. Bella is not happy with Adam because of what he did

I am sure that you can think of others. In pragmatics, these indirectly communicated assumptions are termed 'implicatures' (the term comes from the work of Paul Grice, whose ideas are discussed in the next chapter).

A key feature of implicatures is that they are worked out on the basis not only of what the communicator said, wrote, or signed but also based on assumptions about the context in which they were communicated. As mentioned above, in a different context, an utterance of the expression *I was watching that* would not lead to any of the conclusions in (14).

How do we recognise what counts as an implicature? There has been debate about this, but a common way of thinking about implicatures involves seeing them as conclusions which follow neither from what is directly communicated alone, nor from things we understand from the context, but only from a combination of the two. It does not follow, for example, from the fact that Bella was watching the TV that she wishes Adam hadn't turned it off. For that, we need to make some other assumptions about Bella or about people in general, e.g. that people watch things because they enjoy them and that Bella is likely to have been enjoying the programme and wanting to watch more of it. At the same time, these assumptions alone will not lead to implicatures. We also need to know that Bella has said she was watching the TV. It is the combination of contextual assumptions such as these and what was directly communicated that leads to the implicature.

HOW SURE CAN WE BE OF WHAT BELLA IS COMMUNICATING?

In early discussions of implicatures, it was assumed that indirect communication was fairly simple. A speaker says something and implicates something else. A classic kind of example would be (15):

(15)   Adam: Do you think Calum would like a piece of this cake?
       Bella: He's vegan.

An explanation of what Bella intended might simply say that she directly communicated (16) and implicated (17):

(16)   Calum is vegan at the time at which Bella is speaking
(17)   Calum will not want a piece of cake.

To explain this, we would go on to consider which contextual assumptions interact with (16) to give rise to (17). These might include:

(18)   a.   Vegans do not eat or use anything which involves the exploitation of animal products.
       b.   The cake Adam has asked about contains animal products or things derived from them.

A standard account, putting aside that we need to work out that 'he's vegan' (directly) communicates that Calum has the property of being vegan, might assume that Adam will access the contextual assumption that vegans would not want to eat this cake because it contains things vegans don't eat and assume that this will enable Adam to work out that (Bella thinks that) Calum will not want to eat any of the cake because it contains things he chooses not to eat.

This account also assumes fairly straightforwardly that Bella's utterance implicates this assumption and treats this as 'either/or', i.e. that Bella either implicates this or doesn't. More recent approaches recognise that implicatures can be more or less strongly communicated. On these accounts we can be more or less sure that Bella intends to communicate this rather than this simply being a question of whether she is communicating it or not.

In fact, any implicature can be understood as more or less strongly communicated, and we can understand this more fully by looking at implicatures which are less clear. Returning to the example at the start of this chapter, we might consider how many things Bella's utterance gives evidence for. Here is a list of things she might intend, starting with those mentioned above:

(19)   a.   Bella is unhappy that Adam turned the TV off.
       b.   Bella wanted to carry on watching.

  c. Bella is not happy with Adam because of what he did.
  d. Bella thinks that Adam is insensitive.
  e. Bella thinks that Adam does not care about her feelings or needs.
  f. Adam is thoughtless.
  g. Adam is self-centred.
  h. Adam does not care much about other people.

I expect that some of these seem more plausible than others. Some of them are likely to seem a bit of a stretch. What's important to notice here is that they vary with regard to how strongly we think that Bella is likely to have intended them. We can be very sure of (19a) and (19b), less confident of (19c), less still of (19d) and so on through to (19h), which we can definitely be less sure about and which you might even think is implausible. However, Bella's utterance does provide at least some evidence for (19h). We can see this by asking whether we would be more or less likely to believe it if the only evidence we had was Bella's utterance.

 What this shows is that implicatures can be stronger or weaker rather than just simply communicated or not.

HOW LITERAL IS BELLA BEING?

So far, we have only mentioned in passing the idea that we can use particular expressions more or less literally (in discussing the word *literally*). This is another area where addressees need to make inferences in order to understand what is being communicated.

 Alongside examples such as the colleague I mentioned above who reported receiving 'literally millions of emails', there are lots of loose uses of language. Here are three examples:

  (20) There are 67 million people in the UK.
  (21) Newcastle is 250 miles from Aberdeen.
  (22) Belgium is good for cycling because it's flat.

We wouldn't usually think the speakers here are lying if we find out that (as reported on the Eurostat website where I just checked) there are 66.65 million people in the UK (which is also an approximation, of course), if Aberdeen is 254 miles from Newcastle (also an approximation), or if some parts of Belgium are at a higher altitude than others.

In fact, even cases which seem more straightforward can be understood as more or less literal. When Bella said she 'was watching that', do we assume that she was looking at the TV throughout the time she was sitting in front of it? We would not find it odd if she was looking away now and then or even if she left the room while it was on. She could even have been looking at her phone throughout the time that she was sitting there, maybe listening to (parts of?) the TV programme while doing so. So one thing we need to make assumptions about is how close what has been said is to its literal meaning.

In fact, there are so many cases like this that some theorists question the idea that there is a clear distinction between literal and non-literal uses of language. Instead, the assumption is that utterances can be more or less close to what we would think of as a literal meaning. In many cases, we might not even spend much mental effort to work out how loose or literal an utterance is (Bella's utterance about watching TV could be an example).

Perhaps confusingly, we also talk about non-literal uses when considering both metaphor and irony, even though they work in quite different ways.

IS BELLA BEING METAPHORICAL?

There is a relationship between non-literal utterances and metaphor. Typically, people think of metaphorical utterances as ones where the speaker does not intend what their utterance seems to say but something related in some way. Here are some examples:

(23) Politeness on the London underground is a unicorn.

(24) I tried answering with a joke but it died of neglect before anybody worked out what I meant.

(25) The autopsy showed that my wit died of natural causes. I think a bit of tender loving care could have saved it, though.

Traditionally, metaphorical utterances have been seen as cases where a speaker says something false but intends to communicate something true. Some pragmaticists have seen the true communicated assumption as an implicature. (23) would implicate that politeness does not exist on the London underground, (24) that the audience did not laugh or respond positively to the joke, and (25) extends the idea in (24) and implicates more strongly that the audience did not respond as if this was a joke. In each case, the idea usually is that what is intended shares some properties of what has been said (if taken literally). In (23), politeness on the underground is seen as very rare, as are unicorns. In (24), the joke fell flat in a way which shares some properties with a person or animal dying because it has not received the treatment it needs to keep going or flourish (both of these are themselves metaphorical when thinking about the joke, of course). (25) is a more complicated or sophisticated version of (24), counting on the audience to be quite creative in working out what is meant.

Other approaches argue that the traditional account doesn't work, partly because the implicatures I have just suggested don't seem to capture very well the effects of the metaphorical utterance. In any case, we expect pragmatic theories to be able to explain how metaphorical utterances like these are understood, as well as how addressees work out that they are not intended to be taken literally.

IS BELLA COMMUNICATING HER OWN THOUGHTS?

Another thing we have to work out when understanding utterances is whether the speaker is representing their own thoughts or attributing what they have expressed to somebody else.

Suppose that Calum comes into the room after Adam has turned off the TV in the example above, asks Adam what Bella said, and Adam replies:

(26) I was watching that.

Here, we would be unlikely to assume that Adam is communicating that he was watching something and more likely to think that he is letting Calum know what Bella had said. The first interpretation is possible, though, which shows that we make inferences about this when understanding utterances.

We can report other people's thoughts as well as their utterances. Suppose that Adam asks Bella what Calum thinks of chips and she replies:

(27) They're disgusting.

We might decide that Bella is not answering Adam's question but instead telling him what she (Bella) thinks of chips. If we think Bella is attributing this to Calum, we can assume either that this represents something Calum said or something he thinks. We will also have to make an assumption about how close this is to Calum's utterance or thought. Calum might, for example, have said 'they're disgusting' when asked about chips. He might have said something else (such as 'Chips? Gross!'). Or Bella might be representing what Calum thinks based on a range of utterances or behaviours.

When we report the speech and thoughts of others, we can also indicate that we are doing this, and whether we are representing thoughts or utterances. We might, for example say things like:

(28) She said, 'I was watching that'.
(29) She said she was watching the telly.
(30) He thinks they're disgusting.
(31) He says they're disgusting.

There are lots of examples of more or less close representations of speech and thought in everyday discourse as well as in fiction and other forms of writing. Strictly speaking, we need to work out for every utterance whether the speaker is communicating their own thoughts or reporting somebody else's thoughts or utterance. If we decide it is somebody else's, then we also need to work out how close we think this utterance is to what was originally said, written, or signed.

IS BELLA BEING IRONIC?

Ironical utterances are related to cases where we represent somebody else's speech or thoughts. Classic examples would be cases where a speaker seems to be saying something positive but in fact intends something negative. Suppose, for example, that we have just watched a football match in which the team we support has lost 10-0 and I say:

(32) That went well.

Here, you are likely to decide that I cannot be expressing this positive view and instead decide that I am commenting ironically on the team's terrible performance.

We can also imagine Bella producing an ironic response when Adam turns off the TV she is watching, She might, for example, say one of the following:

(33) Thanks for your concern. I probably do watch too much TV.
(34) Thank you so much for ruining my fun.
(35) Thanks. I probably wouldn't have enjoyed the ending anyway.

Adam is likely to recognise that Bella is not grateful and, as with the non-ironical utterance, that she wishes he hadn't done this.

It would also have been possible for Adam to respond to Bella's utterance ('I was watching that') ironically. Suppose that Adam's and Bella's relationship is not going well and he responds to Bella's utterance above like this:

(36) I was watching that. You're spilling crumbs on the sofa. Do you have to leave the door open? Can I ever do anything right?

Here, we would not assume that Adam is communicating that he was watching anything but instead echoing Bella's utterances (more or less accurately) and intending to convey a negative attitude to them. The final clause here ('Can I ever do anything right?') could be taken to represent a thought of Adam's, but it could also be a representation of a possible thought of Bella's, i.e. he could be attributing a thought like 'can he ever do anything right?' to Bella. If so, again, Adam will need to work out how closely this represents the thought he is attributing to her.

Traditional accounts of irony treat them in a similar way to metaphor, i.e. as cases where the speaker says something false and intends the addressee to infer something true (in some pragmatic accounts, an implicature), usually the opposite of what seems to have been said. In (32), for example, the intention would be to communicate that the match did not go well.

Again, there are other accounts which reject this view, partly because not all ironical utterances can be understood as communicating the opposite of what the speaker has said. In (33)–(35), for example, it's not clear what the opposite would be, and it's not clear that Bella is simply communicating that she is not thanking Adam.

Another issue is that traditional accounts do not explain why speakers produce metaphorical and ironical utterances rather than just saying something like 'Politeness doesn't exist on the London Underground' or 'That didn't go well'. They always seem to communicate more than this. An alternative sees ironical utterances as related to cases where the speaker represents somebody else's speech or thoughts as well as that the speaker has a negative attitude to these thoughts.

WHAT ABOUT HOW BELLA SAYS HER UTTERANCE?

As mentioned above, understanding is also affected by how we say things. What I have in mind here is technically called 'prosody'. It refers to all aspects of the way the utterance sounds (in speech) or is signed (in sign language) other than those involved in working out what linguistic forms Bella is using (or representing through her speech sounds). Key things in speech include pitch movement, rhythm, pace, volume, and voice quality. For example, Adam will understand Bella's utterance differently if she says it with a falling pitch or a rising pitch. (I have indicated these here with a rising line for rising pitch and a falling one for a falling pitch, without worrying about other details, such as whether they begin and end high or low compared to the rest of Bella's speech).

(37) I was \ watching that.
(38) I was / watching that.

A common but incorrect assumption is that, in English, falling pitch is associated with statements and rising pitch with questions. In fact, we can ask questions with falling pitch and make statements with rising pitch.

We can also affect understanding by the speed and rhythm at which we speak. One way of producing utterances is often indicated with full stops where they wouldn't usually appear inside clauses:

(39) I. Was. Watching. That.

In English, pausing after each word and keeping to a strict rhythm has significant consequences for interpretations, which are quite different from producing a very fast utterance where the syllables are close together in a more continuous stream.

We can also affect interpretations by changing the volume of our utterances (shouting or speaking quietly) or our voice quality (whispering or using a 'creaky' voice).

So it is not just the words we use which help us to understand each other.

WHAT ABOUT BELLA'S NONVERBAL BEHAVIOUR?

Communication is also affected by nonverbal behaviour. If Bella speaks with her head bowed and hardly moving, Adam (if he looks at her) will understand the utterance differently from how he would take it if Bella leapt to her feet, threw her arms to the side, and raised her eyebrows.

As well as nonverbal behaviour accompanying speech, we can communicate only nonverbally, i.e. without speaking at all. Bella might, for example, make a nonverbal sound (e.g. a high-pitched noise with no discernible linguistic content indicating unhappiness, a sigh, or a loud cough) or she might do something else, such as standing up and leaving the room with shoulders slumped. Or she might stand and tower over Adam in a pretend menacing way.

While accounting for the meanings of nonverbal behaviour in general is not usually seen as a task for pragmatic theories, we do expect them to explain how we work out from those meanings what is intended in specific contexts.

HOW DO ADAM AND BELLA CONSTRUCT MEANINGS TOGETHER?

In 'early' (i.e. mid to late twentieth century) work in pragmatics, discussion often focused on individual turns in an interaction, e.g. just Bella's utterance in this interaction, as we have been doing here. It also often focused mainly on how addressees (Adam here) worked out what they think the communicator (Bella) intended.

However, communication does not involve just a series of individual turns, and communicators do not simply provide turns which addressees then interpret. Rather, interpretation extends over a number of turns (with interpretation sometimes carrying on after the interaction) and communicators work together to 'negotiate' or 'co-construct' communication.

Pragmatic theories should explain how what is communicated follows from the behaviour of everybody who is interacting and how it can carry on after the immediate interaction.

We can see how communication is collaborative by thinking about how Adam responds to Bella's utterance and how she responds to that. Imagine, for example, if Adam responded to Bella's utterance by apologising straight away, maybe with some nonverbal behaviour to indicate surprise and regret. Bella might then respond quite positively to that, as in the continued exchange in (40):

(40) Adam: Oh, I'm really sorry, I didn't see you there! I'll put it on again. *(He switches the TV back on.)*

Bella: Thanks. Don't worry. I was only half paying attention anyway.

Or she might respond more negatively to this as here:

(41) Adam: Oh, I'm really sorry, I didn't see you there! I'll put it on again. *(He switches the TV back on).*

Bella: Sure you didn't. *(Pause.)* You're always doing things like this! *(She walks out.)*

In the first case, Bella clearly accepts Adam's apology, tells him not to worry about it, and indicates that the interruption of her viewing is not as serious as it would have been if she had been following the programme really closely. In the second case, she makes clear that she does not think his apology is serious and suggests that it follows a pattern where Adam doesn't take what Bella wants seriously. We'll consider in Chapter 5 how things we do when communicating can contribute to making interactions more or less polite or impolite. For now, notice that the nature of the interaction is determined not just by one of the people involved but by what they both do and how they respond to each other. It also arises from the whole sequence of utterances and not just from each utterance individually.

We can still talk, of course, about what an individual intends by what they say and do as well as about how an individual understands what others say or do (even though both of these might not be fully clear, even to the individuals themselves), but we also need to recognise how they work together to create communication and understanding.

AN IMPORTANT GAP

Many theorists and others who have discussed how we communicate and understand each other in specific situations have identified some of the aspects of what is involved:

a. linguistic expressions with specific meanings
b. nonverbal behaviour, some with specific meanings
c. contextual assumptions which affect how we make inferences
d. inferences involved in working out what is directly communicated
e. inferences involved in working out what is indirectly communicated

If we can identify each of these things, we go some way towards explaining how communicative behaviour is produced and understood. As I mentioned above, early work focused mainly on how we understand communicative acts. Going back to the example at the start of this chapter, we can say the following about Bella's utterance (making some assumptions about how Bella said it and the context):

a. Bella produced sounds which represent the linguistic forms *I was watching that*
b. Bella said this with prosody and nonverbal behaviour suggesting that she is surprised and unhappy
c. Adam and Bella can access contextual assumptions including that Bella was in the room when Adam came in, that Adam turned off the TV, and that people who are watching something on TV want the TV to remain switched on
d. Adam infers that Bella is communicating that Bella was watching something on the TV which Adam has just turned off
e. Adam infers that Bella is upset that he has turned off the TV and that she wants it turned on again

If we say all of this, we have left a big gap in our explanation. We have said nothing about what guides Adam to make these inferences, i.e. about how exactly Adam works out what Bella is communicating directly and indirectly. While the interpretation Adam goes for might seem obvious, we need to explain what leads him in this direction rather than towards other possibilities. Why, for example, does he not think that she is saying she was watching something else, and how does he know that she wishes he hadn't turned it off and would like it turned on again? In the next chapter, we will look at ideas proposed by Paul Grice which are generally acknowledged as the first significant proposal made for how we can explain this.

FINDING OUT MORE

Here are some ideas for things you might do to develop understanding of ideas in the chapter and to find out more, followed by some suggested further reading.

YOUR OWN EXAMPLES

It's always helpful to notice and try to explain your own examples. So look out for and make notes of any interesting examples you come across and see if you can relate them to ideas in each chapter of the book. For this chapter, the main thing to focus on is how things other than linguistic meanings are involved in interaction and the kinds of inferences you think have been made by people involved. You can also consider each of the things discussed in the chapter which pragmatics aims to explain. To see how well you understand each one, try to come up with examples (real or invented) of your own which you could use to explain them to somebody else.

MISUNDERSTANDINGS

Make a note of any cases where you misunderstand communicative acts or where other people do. See if you can pinpoint the source of misunderstanding and if you can refer to ideas from this chapter to help explain things.

EXAMPLES FROM MEDIA

Keep your eyes and ears open for examples in film, TV, literature, adverts, newspapers, etc. Look out for examples which reveal something about communication. Again, see if you can refer to ideas from this chapter to help explain things.

ARTIFICIAL COMMUNICATION

To help you think about all of the complexities involved in human communication, look at examples where machines 'communicate' artificially, e.g. the virtual assistant on a smartphone or recorded options when you call a business number. What does the machine do which is different from what a human would be likely to do?

FACE-TO-FACE AND OTHER KINDS OF COMMUNICATION

Compare face-to-face communication with other kinds, e.g. with email, text messages, social message services online. What kinds of things do we do for each type of communication and how are they different from each other? (To take one example, the pitch of our voices can change when speaking but not when typing.) Some researchers have suggested that some of the things we do when texting or emailing aim to perform functions similar to things like intonation, facial movements, or body language. Consider some of these different options and their effects.

FURTHER READING

There's a lot of writing and research on pragmatics and so you could spend a lot of time reading about it. Luckily, there are also some very good textbooks. Here are some suggestions to get you started. The ones I have chosen here are accessible and have useful examples. As many tutors and students nowadays look for recent references, it's worth pointing out that the books with earlier publication dates (by Stephen Levinson, Jenny Thomas, and Jean Stilwell Peccei) are all very clear and still useful.

1. Birner, Betty J. 2012. *Introduction to Pragmatics*, Wiley-Blackwell.
2. Chapman, Siobhan. 2011. *Pragmatics*. Palgrave Macmillan.
3. Culpeper, Jonathan and Michael Haugh. 2014. *Pragmatics and the English Language*. Palgrave Macmillan. (A useful introduction to ideas about pragmatics, even though, like this book, it focuses on English varieties).
4. Cummins, Chris. 2019. *Pragmatics*. Edinburgh University Press.
5. Cutting, Joan and Kenneth Fordyce. 2020. *Pragmatics: A Resource Book for Students*, 4th edition. Routledge.
6. Grundy, Peter. 2019. *Doing Pragmatics*, 4th edition. Routledge.

7.   Huang, Yan. 2014. *Pragmatics*, 2nd edition. Oxford University Press.

8.   Levinson, Stephen C. 1983. *Pragmatics*. Cambridge University Press.

9.   O'Keeffe, Anne, Brian Clancy and Svenja Adolphs. 2019. *Introducing Pragmatics in Use*. Routledge.

10.   Peccei, Jean Stillwell. 1999. *Pragmatics*. Routledge.

11.   Thomas, Jenny. 1995. *Meaning in Interaction*. Routledge.

MEANING MORE THAN WE SAY
GRICE'S SUGGESTION

Most work in pragmatics today ultimately derives from ideas developed by the philosopher Paul Grice in the mid-twentieth century. This chapter discusses his most influential ideas. Responding to issues with these led to the development of more recent approaches, including the 'neo-Gricean' approaches discussed in Chapter 3 and the 'post-Gricean' approach, relevance theory, discussed in Chapter 4.

RATIONALITY AND MEANING

One of Grice's most important contributions was to suggest a way to fill the gap mentioned at the end of Chapter 1, i.e. to suggest what guides us in working out meanings in contexts. One way of describing Grice's focus is to say that it is on how we sometimes 'mean more than we say'. We can illustrate with this example from Chapter 1:

> (1) Adam: Do you think Calum would like a piece of this cake?
> Bella: He's vegan.

As we said, Bella is not simply informing Adam here that Calum is vegan. She is letting Adam know that Calum will not want a piece of cake (because he is vegan).

In other contexts, the same utterance can mean something else:

(2) Adam: I don't think I've ever met anyone who's less aware of the climate emergency than Calum is. Does he ever do anything that's good for the planet?

    Bella:　He's vegan.

(3) Adam: I've been asked to find a friendly vegan for a podcast. Would you say Calum's a friendly vegan?

    Bella:　He's vegan.

In (2), Adam will think that Calum might care about the climate crisis after all (given that caring about the planet is one reason for choosing to be vegan). In (3), Adam is likely to think that Adam is not friendly or at least that Bella does not know whether he is.

While the possibility of the same expression meaning different things in different contexts was discussed at least as long ago as ancient Greece, there was no credible suggestion of how this happens until Grice made his suggestion, which is that there are underlyingly rational principles which lead to the different interpretations. We will look at the details of Grice's proposal below. For now, notice that we can say something about how Adam understands these utterances by considering what it would be rational for him to assume.

In example (1), Adam has asked about whether Calum will want some cake. If we assume that Bella is interested in giving Adam the kind of answer he expects, it would not be rational just to tell Adam something about Calum and not to communicate anything about whether he might want cake. If Adam assumes that Bella will want to answer the question, he can assume that she might be expecting him to access some contextual assumptions and use them to arrive at something she is indirectly communicating which does answer the question.

We can suggest similar explanations based on thinking about what would be rational when thinking about (2) and (3). In (2), Adam is talking about Calum and saying he doesn't seem to care about the climate crisis. Would it be rational for Bella just to say something about Adam which doesn't connect with this? If we assume not, then we might look for something she is indirectly communicating which does relate to what Adam has said. Her utterance seems rational if we assume that she is offering indirect evidence that maybe Calum does care about climate issues after all.

In (3), Adam has indicated that he wants to know whether Calum counts as a friendly vegan. If Bella thought so, she could have simply said 'yes' (maybe with a few more words for politeness reasons). It would not be rational to choose to say only that he's vegan if she also thinks he's friendly. If Adam thinks that Bella is a rational communicator, then he is likely to assume either that she thinks Calum is not friendly or that she doesn't know whether he is. The exciting idea here is that we can propose rational principles which explain how we communicate more than the linguistic meanings of expressions we use in utterances.

TYPES OF MEANING

Another very important contribution made by Grice was his discussion of different kinds of meaning. As we saw in Chapter 1, the word *meaning* has many different senses. Grice considered several of these and proposed an important and influential distinction between 'natural' meaning and 'non-natural' meaning (or 'meaning$_{NN}$'). This distinction is important, as cases of non-natural meaning are where the rational principles proposed by Grice play a role.

'Natural' meaning is where we know something follows because of what we know about how the world works. A classic example is the idea that smoke 'means' fire, i.e. that seeing smoke means we can infer that there must be a fire somewhere causing the smoke. 'Non-natural' meaning is where something follows because humans intend them to mean those things. Two examples Grice discussed (among others) were:

(4) Those spots mean measles.
(5) Those three rings on the bell mean the bus is full.

The spots indicate measles in that they are a symptom of them and somebody with those spots must have measles. The example of the three rings on the bell come from a time when buses had conductors who rang a bell once to ask the driver to stop, twice when it was safe to leave a stop, and three times to mean the bus was full and nobody needed to get off so that there was no need to stop at the next bus stop.

One of several differences between them pointed out by Grice is that it would be odd to deny that the person with spots had measles but not that the bus was full:

(6) Those spots mean measles but in fact she doesn't have measles.

(7) Those three rings on the bell mean the bus is full but the bus isn't really full. The conductor's made a mistake.

(6) sounds odd because the second clause contradicts the first one. (7) sounds fine because it's possible for the conductor to have meant to communicate something but to be mistaken.

One reason that the distinction between natural and non-natural meaning is important is because the rational principles which Grice envisaged as guiding communication apply to cases of non-natural meaning but not to natural meaning. We can understand that smoke means fire or that certain spots mean measles just by seeing them. For non-natural meaning, we need to think about what a communicator intended and what it would be rational to communicate.

To take an everyday example, consider two ways Bella might respond in this exchange:

(8) Adam: Are you sure you're OK to teach today? Has your cold cleared up?
    Bella: a. To be honest, I've been better.
           b. *(with a croaky voice)* Yeh, I'm fine.

Hearing the first possible response, Adam can assume that Bella is not completely better and that she maybe shouldn't be teaching. This is because her utterance reveals her intention to communicate this. This is a case of non-natural meaning and we can explain it by referring to rational principles. Hearing the second response, Adam will recognise that Bella is communicating (non-naturally) that she's fine. He might also make some inferences based on her croaky voice (and maybe other clues, like what she looks like). If he does, these follow just from Adam's perception of Bella, and these are natural meanings. Adam can integrate the natural and non-natural meanings here to conclude that Bella is saying she's fine but doesn't seem very well to him.

It's also possible, of course, that Bella could intentionally communicate something using a croaky voice. She might, for example, just make a croaky sound or something like a cough. In this case, this would be a case of non-natural meaning and Adam would decide that Bella is trying to communicate that she's not very well.

PRINCIPLES AND MAXIMS

So what are the principles which Grice suggested to account for how we understand each other in cases of non-natural meaning? First, he suggested that there is a sense in which communication is cooperative behaviour. Communicators are cooperating in working together to establish what is being communicated. He recognised that we sometimes do uncooperative things such as lying or aiming to deceive each other, but he suggested that communication involves the shared goal of getting communication to happen. He also assumed that certain things would be rational to do when two or more people are working towards a shared goal.

With this in mind, Grice proposed a general and overarching Cooperative Principle and a number of more specific 'maxims of conversation' which are subsumed within it, as represented in Figure 2.1.

One way to begin to understand Grice's approach is to consider each maxim in turn.

MAXIMS OF QUANTITY

The maxims of quantity say that we should aim to make our contribution as informative as is required and not more than that. Intuitively, it seems reasonable to assume that communicators aim to provide enough information but not too much. We can illustrate this by imagining utterances which seem to give more or less information than we expect. Consider these two exchanges:

  (9) Adam: What is the exam for this module like?
       Bella: Like an exam.
  (10) Adam: What is the exam for this module like?
       Bella: It starts with all the students gathering on campus outside the exam room. Then an invigilator opens the door and invites everybody into the room...

Intuitively, most people I have spoken to about examples like this see that Bella's answer in (9) is not informative enough, as it only tells Adam that the exam shares some properties with exams, which of course he already knows. The answer in (10), by contrast, is too

---

Grice's Cooperative Principle and Maxims of Conversation

Cooperative Principle:

Make your conversational contribution such as is required, at the stage at which it occurs, by the accepted purpose or direction of the talk exchange in which you are engaged.

Maxims of Quantity:

1.   Make your contribution as informative as is required (for the current purposes of the exchange)

2.   Do not make your contribution more informative than is required.

Maxims of Quality:

1.   Do not say what you believe to be false

2.   Do not say that for which you have inadequate evidence

Maxim of Relation:

Be relevant

Maxims of Manner:

1.   Avoid obscurity of expression

2.   Avoid ambiguity

3.   Be brief (avoid unnecessaryprolixity)

4.   Be orderly.

FIGURE 2.1 Grice's Cooperative Principle and Maxims of Conversation (adapted from Grice 1975: 45–46)

informative, including details which Adam is already likely to be aware of and which Bella does not need to repeat for him here.

While we have intuitions like this about what seems under-informative or over-informative, most people will not simply assume that

Bella's utterances here have failed to communicate something useful. Instead, they will assume that she is saying too little or too much for a reason. In (9), we are likely to think that she is rudely refusing to give a clear answer, perhaps also implicating that she thinks Alex is stupid or should know that she doesn't know more than him about the exam. In (10), she is again likely to be seen as rude and unhelpful, perhaps suggesting that she thinks Alex is so stupid that he needs to have really obvious things spelled out for him. In the cake example above, the information that Calum is vegan is not, on its own, informative enough. Adam recognises this and this is why he assumes that she intends more and infers that Bella means that Calum won't want cake because he is vegan.

MAXIMS OF QUALITY

The maxims of quality are about truthfulness. They say that we should not say things we think are false and not say things for which we don't have adequate evidence. While Grice did not assume that people necessarily tell the truth when communicating with each other (for example, he discussed cases of lying), he did assume that we aim to be taken as truthful and that people we communicate with assume that we are presenting what we say as truthful. If somebody says something clearly false, we recognise this and attempt to come up with an explanation, e.g. that the utterance is ironic or metaphorical.

MAXIM OF RELATION

The maxim of relation simply says that we should 'be relevant'. Grice recognised a problem with this maxim, which is that we would need to have a definition of the term *relevant* for it to be useful. He never got round to developing a fuller definition so we have either to assume a fairly intuitive understanding, where it is roughly about 'connecting with' the topic being discussed, or come up with our own definition. Other pragmaticists have discussed how the term can be defined, and one approach, relevance theory, includes a proposed technical definition of the term.

Even without a clear definition, most people would agree that we seem to expect utterances to be 'relevant' in some way. Consider this example:

(11) Adam: How you getting on with your pragmatics essay?
      Bella: It's a beautiful day, isn't it? Look at that sky!

Bella's utterance is not directly relevant to the question which Adam has asked. As with other examples, we can imagine things which Bella could be intending to communicate by producing an utterance which does not seem to follow the maxim, e.g. that she is not getting on well with the pragmatics essay and that she would rather not talk about it.

MAXIMS OF MANNER

The maxims of manner are different from the others in that they are about the form or the semantic/pragmatic properties of utterances, i.e. about which expressions we choose to use and what they mean.

The first maxim of manner suggests that we should not use obscure expressions, e.g. we should not use an expression like *the ingestion of liquid matter* when we could use something more straightforward such as *drinking*.

The second maxim suggests that we should avoid ambiguity. It's important to notice here that Grice is using the term *ambiguity* in a sense different from that most commonly used by linguists. Rather than referring to the use of expressions which have more than one linguistic meaning (which it would be almost impossible to avoid), he means that we should avoid expressions where we cannot work out in context what they mean. So it's fine to use an ambiguous expression like *mug* when it is clear what sense is intended (e.g. saying 'I've made you a mug of soup') but not where it is not easy to work out which sense must be intended.

The third maxim says that we should not use unnecessarily long formulations, e.g. saying 'he moved his facial features in a way that indicates amusement' where we could say 'he smiled' (note that this can also be seen as violating the first maxim of manner by being obscure).

The fourth maxim says to be orderly. It's not clear to what extent we follow this idea in general. We often, for example, start telling a story by saying something about what happens later in the story and then coming back to talk about earlier moments (this is also common in fiction and drama, of course). One case where this maxim has been referred to is in using conjunctions like *she read a story and went to bed.*

We would usually assume that she first read the story and then went to bed.

The maxims of manner have not been referred to much in explanations of utterances. Grice gave a few examples, including someone saying (12) rather than (13) when describing a singer's performance:

> (12) She produced a series of sounds that corresponded closely with the score of 'Home Sweet Home'.
> (13) She sang 'Home Sweet Home'.

Grice suggests that the unnecessarily long utterance in (12) would implicate that there was something about the performance which was different from what we usually describe as *singing*, i.e. that it was not a good or enjoyable performance.

The assumption that rational principles like this govern communication and can explain how we understand each other in context was a huge breakthrough. Another key part of Grice's account was the distinction he suggested between saying and implicating.

SAYING AND IMPLICATING

A fundamental distinction proposed by Grice is between what an utterance *says* and what it *implicates*. It is because of the notion of implicature that Grice can suggest an account of how we can 'mean more than we say'. For Grice, we do this by implicating things.

The essential distinction is intuitively quite clear (even if there are complications when we look at the details). I characterised it above as a distinction between what we communicate directly and what we communicate indirectly. When Bella says that Calum is vegan above, she can be seen as *saying* that Calum is vegan and as *implicating* that he won't want any cake. Here are some more examples:

> (14) Adam: Do you want to come and see the new *Mission Impossible* film tonight?
> Bella: I don't like action films.
> *What is said:*
> Bella doesn't like action films.
> *What is implicated:*

>Bella doesn't want to see the new *Mission Impossible* film tonight.

(15) Adam: Should we bring Dani some biscuits?

>Bella: There's gluten in them.
>
>*What is said:*
>
>There is gluten in the biscuits Adam is thinking of bringing to Dani.
>
>*What is implicated:*
>
>We shouldn't bring the biscuits to Dani.

The key idea here probably seems clear but we should notice that our characterisation of 'what is said' each time involves words which are not identical to those in the original utterance. In fact, we have assumed some pragmatic inference in order to arrive at what is said. In Chapter 1 we looked at some of the things that need to be inferred in order to work out what is directly communicated ('said', for Grice) and of course these apply here. However, Grice did not say much about inferences like these, and recognising the role of pragmatics in working out what is said is one significant development in approaches which build on Grice's work.

TYPES OF IMPLICATURE

So far we have seen that Grice made a distinction between saying and implicating and that he did not say much about how we arrive at what is said. The picture we have developed so far is summarised in Figure 2.2.

This figure shows that linguistic communication involves both saying and implicating. We could add some further information at the top of the figure, distinguishing different kinds of communication (linguistic and non-linguistic, intentional and unintentional)

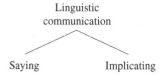

FIGURE 2.2 Grice's saying-implicating distinction

but for now we will focus on further subdivisions proposed by Grice with regard to implicature. This leads to a new picture, represented in Figure 2.3.

As the figure shows, Grice proposed that there are three types of implicature. The variety that has by far received the most focus is what he termed 'particularised conversational implicatures', which arise in specific situations and given specific contextual assumptions. We have looked at several examples of these already. When Bella says that Calum is vegan and this implicates that he won't want any of the cake Adam is referring to, this follows in the specific context in which Bella utters it but not every time anybody utters the linguistic expression *he's vegan*. If the conversation was about Dani, then it would implicate that Dani wouldn't want any. If it was about biscuits, it would implicate he wouldn't want any biscuits. And so on.

Grice proposed two other kinds of implicature. He first distinguished what he called 'conventional implicature', which he saw as following from the meanings of words used, from conversational implicature, which depended on contextual assumptions and the maxims of conversation. He then subdivided conversational implicatures into 'generalised' ones, which would usually follow from saying something, from 'particularised' ones, which only followed in a specific context.

Students often find it difficult to distinguish the three kinds of implicature (I was confused when I first studied Grice's ideas) so I

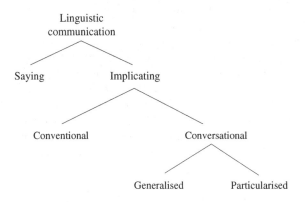

FIGURE 2.3 Grice's view of linguistic communication

will be systematic here, beginning with a brief description and some examples of each type and then presenting a checklist which should help to identify which type of implicature we are considering in particular situations.

CONVENTIONAL IMPLICATURE

These are implicatures which follow from the meanings of the words used and do not depend on the maxims or aspects of the context. The idea is that some linguistic expressions give rise to a particular type of implicature every time they are used (regardless of the context).

A number of words which can connect clauses in English, such as *so* and *but*, have been seen as examples of 'conventional implicature'. Here is an utterance containing representations of two clauses with no conventional implicature term and so no indication of how they are connected:

(16) Dani is a teenager. She's full of energy.

Hearers might infer any of a number of relationships, and different contextual assumptions will make different inferences about this more likely. Speakers also have the option of including linguistic expressions (connectives) which affect this:

(17) Dani is a teenager so she's full of energy.
(18) Dani is a teenager but she's full of energy.

The use of *so* suggests that it is not surprising that Dani is full of energy given that she's a teenager (suggesting, therefore, that the speaker expects teenagers to be full of energy). The use of *but* suggests that her energy is surprising given that she's a teenager (suggesting, therefore, that the speaker does not expect teenagers to be full of energy).

For Grice, conventional implicatures differ from conversational implicatures in that they are linguistically 'encoded' and do not depend on aspects of the context. A key difference is that conversational implicatures can be cancelled either because something in the context rules them out or by the speaker saying something to cancel them explicitly, as here:

(19) He's vegan. He's not very strict about it, though, so he might taste the cake.

If Bella gave this response to a question about Calum wanting cake, we can see the second part as cancelling a possible implicature (that Calum won't want any cake) from the first part.

This is not possible for conventional implicatures:

(20) Dani is a teenager but she's full of energy. Not that I think teenagers aren't full of energy or anything.

Hearers or readers of this utterance are likely to think that the second part of the utterance is ironic or just that the utterance doesn't make sense. It doesn't seem possible to use *but* like this and then immediately to contradict the conclusion suggested by having used it (unless the first bit is understood as something another person has said and you are now seen as contradicting them).

While it seems clear that expressions like this do have unusual kinds of linguistic meanings, there has been considerable discussion about exactly what they mean and how, as well as about the notion of conventional implicature itself, with many theorists not adopting the idea.

GENERALISED CONVERSATIONAL IMPLICATURE

Grice also proposed a distinction between two types of conversational implicature. 'Particularised conversational implicatures' are context-specific implicatures which arise because of particular aspects of the context. He also identified implicatures which, he suggested, usually arise when a certain 'form of words' is used unless something specifically cancels them. He called these 'generalised conversational implicatures', suggesting that:

[s]ometimes one can say that the use of a certain form of words in an utterance would normally (in the ABSENCE of special circumstances) carry such-and-such an implicature or type of implicature.

(Grice 1975: 56)

Grice's first example for this was the case of someone saying '*X is meeting a woman tonight*'. The implicature Grice had in mind was that the woman is not in a close relationship with X, e.g. his wife, sister, or best friend. Here are two more examples:

(21) I had to sit next to a noisy eater at the cinema yesterday.

(22) I broke a finger yesterday.

In the first example, we are likely to assume that the noisy eater is not the speaker's friend or relative. In the second (one of Grice's examples), we assume that the finger is one of the speaker's own fingers (biologically attached to his hand). A character played by the comedian Groucho Marx exploited this kind of reasoning when he said as he left a party:

(23) I've had a perfectly wonderful evening.

And then went on to say:

(24) But this wasn't it.

Where do these implicatures come from? First, notice that in the three cases above (before the Groucho Marx example), I did not need to offer any information about who was saying this and in what situation. I gave no contextual gloss or previous utterance which the speaker was seen as responding to. Grice suggested that these were 'generalised' implicatures because they typically follow from using this form of words rather than requiring specific contextual features to give rise to them (which is the case for 'particularised' conversational implicatures).

While they don't depend on specific aspects of the context, generalised conversational implicatures are context-dependent as we can imagine contexts where they would not be derived. Suppose that I go to the cinema with a friend and then somebody else talks to us about how annoying it is when somebody eats noisily in the cinema. If my friend then says (21) in this context, I will infer that she means me. (22) might give rise to a different implicature if the speaker has a job which involves making pottery figures of humans or human hands. In this context, we are likely to assume that she broke one of the fingers she was making.

We can also cancel generalised conversational implicatures explicitly by saying that we don't intend them, as the Groucho Marx character did in (24), e.g. we might say:

(25) I had to sit next to a noisy eater at the cinema yesterday. My boyfriend!

(26) I broke a finger yesterday. Not one of my own. It was part of
      a porcelain figure.

 The fact that we can cancel implicatures like this shows that they do
not depend only on the meanings of linguistic expressions. Therefore
they are conversational implicatures. The fact that they typically
occur when these expressions are used means that they are 'generalised' rather than 'particularised'.

 How are the maxims involved? As with several of Grice's accounts,
the view here is slightly complicated in that it involves thinking about
how things might have been different. The idea here is that the speaker
would be violating some of the maxims if they did not intend the implicature. If you are talking about your wife, then you could use the expression *my wife*. This is more informative than *a woman* and so you would
not be being 'informative enough' (i.e. observing the first maxim of
quantity) if you said *a woman* and intended to refer to your wife. (Note,
by the way, that, as always, this is about what is intentionally communicated. It could that the woman is the speaker's wife but speakers will not
be taken to mean that if they use the expression *a woman*).

 There have been criticisms of the notion of generalised conversational implicature as Grice originally presented it, including disagreement about whether we need this separate category, but it has been
very influential.

PARTICULARISED CONVERSATIONAL IMPLICATURE

As I said, the first examples we've looked at in this chapter are what
Grice called 'particularised conversational implicatures'. These follow
from specific aspects of the context. They depend on the maxims and
on specific contextual assumptions. They would not arise in general
from using the particular linguistic expressions which generate them in
specific contexts. We can see that an implicature is 'particularised' by
presenting the utterance which gives rise to it without any indication
of specific contextual assumptions (or an immediately preceding
utterance):

(27) He's vegan.
(28) It's a beautiful day, isn't it?
(29) I'm assuming that you like big empty spaces.

Without any information on when these were uttered, we cannot guess much about what they are likely to implicate. We looked at some options for *he's vegan* above. Here are two options for the other two utterances, with one potential implicature indicated for each example:

(30) Adam: I'm thinking of going for a walk this morning.
      Bella: It's a beautiful day, isn't it?
              Possible implicature:
              It's a good idea to go for a walk.

(31) Adam: How are you getting on with your essay?
      Bella: It's a beautiful day, isn't it?
              Possible implicature:
              Work on the essay is not going well.

(32) Adam: I'm thinking of going hiking in the Australian outback.
      Bella: I'm assuming that you like big empty spaces.
              Possible implicature:
              Your plan is a good one if you like big empty spaces.

(33) Adam: I'm thinking of inviting Calum to my party on Saturday.
      Bella: I'm assuming that you like big empty spaces.
              Possible implicature:
              If you invite Calum, lots of the other people you invite won't come or will leave soon after they arrive.

Each of the suggested implicatures above only arises given that there are specific contextual assumptions which interact with what the speaker has said. Particularised implicatures arise from the interaction of linguistic meanings and specific contextual assumptions while generalised implicatures typically arise unless specific contextual assumptions cancel them.

To summarise, Table 2.1 lists properties of saying and the three types of implicature.

It is not easy to use Grice's approach and to be clear on what kind of communicated assumptions we are dealing with each time. I believe that this follows partly because we do not usually think explicitly about how we are working out what people communicate and partly because some of Grice's examples and some of the kinds of thinking

TABLE 2.1 Properties of saying and three types of implicature

	Saying	Conventional implicature	Generalised conversational implicature	Particularised conversational implicature
Linguistically encoded?	Yes	Yes	No	No
Involve pragmatic inference?	Yes, but Grice didn't discuss this	No	Yes	Yes
Depend on context?	Yes, but Grice didn't discuss this	No	Yes. They arise as long as features of the context do not rule them out	Yes. They only arise given specific features of the context
Maxims involved in deriving them?	Not for Grice, but later approaches claim pragmatic principles are involved	No	Yes. The speaker would be violating the maxims if they did not intend the implicature	Yes. The speaker would be violating the maxims if they did not intend the implicature
Cancellable?	No but the context can affect what is said and speakers can explicitly indicate what they intend, e.g. 'when I said *we* I was referring to…'	No	Yes	Yes

involved in deriving conclusions seem less natural than others. This might partly follow from Grice's experience being in a particular time and context, which is not close to those of current students and others. However, it is possible to develop an understanding by looking at examples and working through them. And the most important contribution Grice made here is to show that we can fill a gap in our explanation of how we understand each other by assuming that rational principles guide our understanding.

USING THE MAXIMS

There are a number of ways in which the maxims play a role in an account of the two kinds of conversational implicatures. It's also possible to violate maxims without giving rise to implicatures. This happens when it is not clear to addressees that a maxim is being violated.

In discussing what gives rise to implicatures, Grice identified three cases: cases where no maxim is violated, cases where a maxim is violated because of a 'clash' of maxims (the speaker couldn't observe one maxim without violating another), and cases which are often referred to (including by Grice) as 'flouting', where a maxim is blatantly violated in order to give rise to an implicature.

NO IMPLICATURES VIOLATED

Grice's examples of cases where no maxim is violated are both arguably problematic. Here they are (with names and places changed):

(34) Adam: I'm out of petrol.
      Bella: There's a garage around the corner.
(35) Adam: Calum doesn't seem to have a girlfriend these days.
      Bella: He's been going to Darlington a lot lately.

For cases like (34), Grice suggests the implicature that (as far as Bella knows) the garage is open with petrol on sale. In (35), the implicature is that Calum might have a girlfriend in Darlington.

A problem with (34), acknowledged by Grice, is that the implicature is not one that people usually notice or comment on. I would argue that it is nevertheless reasonable to suggest that the utterance implicates something like this. In the spirit of Grice's approach, the reasoning is that Bella would be being under-informative if she thinks the garage is closed or out of petrol (she would, of course, be being misleading if so). If challenged, it would be hard for Bella to claim plausibly that she didn't intend this.

The problem with (35) is that it seems equally possible to suggest that the speaker expects the hearer to see that what she has said is not relevant or informative enough on its own and so that it is necessary to derive an implicature which makes the utterance as a whole relevant and informative. Knowing about Calum's travel on its own says nothing about whether he has a girlfriend and so the implicature is necessary. On this view, this is an example of 'flouting' a maxim (discussed below).

Grice did not make an explicit link between these cases and cases of generalised conversational implicature but this seems like a natural connection to make. If I say (36) to you:

(36) I saw a beautiful house yesterday.

you are likely to assume that the house is not my own house. If I intended to tell you about my own house, I should have been more informative and used an expression which made this clear. No maxim is violated by (36) but a maxim would be being violated if I had not intended this. On Grice's approach, all generalised conversational implicatures would be explained in this way. This follows from his statement that generalised conversational implicatures arise 'normally (in the ABSENCE of special circumstances)' and not because of 'special features of the context'.

WHEN MAXIMS 'CLASH'

A clash of maxims occurs where observing one maxim would involve the violation of another. An example (adapted from one of Grice's) is:

(37) Adam: Where does Dani live?
      Bella: Somewhere in the Borders.

Adam might think that Bella's utterance on its own is not informative enough as it only identifies an area (in the south of Scotland) without naming a particular town which Dani lives in or near to. However, he is likely to assume that she has been under-informative because she does not know exactly where Dani lives. An appropriately informative utterance would violate the second maxim of quantity by saying something for which she lacks adequate evidence.

This is another kind of example which often seems counterintuitive. Again, my view is that Bella's utterance does give evidence for the assumption that she doesn't know exactly where Dani lives and so that this is an implicature of the utterance. However, it is not a very salient one and hearers might not report it if asked to say what Bella communicated.

'FLOUTING' MAXIMS

Cases of flouting are the ones most often discussed when thinking about Grice's approach, partly, I think, because they are fairly intuitive and easy to grasp (as long as we pick cases where there is only one clear implicature or a fairly small number of them). In these cases, the speaker says something which clearly violates at least one maxim at the level of what is said with the expectation that the hearer can derive an implicature which makes the utterance as a whole consistent with the maxims.

We have looked at several examples which fall into this pattern. Here are two of them again:

(38) Adam: What is the exam for this module like?
        Bella: Like an exam.
(39) Adam: How you getting on with your pragmatics essay?
        Bella: It's a beautiful day, isn't it? Look at that sky!

In these cases, we can think of Bella as saying something which is clearly not informative enough. Adam can see that what she has said is not informative enough and so he looks for an implicature which would make the utterance as a whole informative enough. The implicatures are that Bella does not want to tell Adam about the exam (and maybe that she thinks he is stupid or annoying) and that Bella does not want to talk about her essay (which must not be going well).

These used to be the most-often discussed kinds of examples when discussing Grice's work (questions about the pragmatics of saying and generalised conversational implicatures have been discussed more fully in more recent theoretical debates). I think that this is because it is easier to grasp the idea here and also because we are more aware of these kinds of inferences. In some ways, though, this makes them less interesting than cases where our intuitions are less clear. Arguably, there is something marked about particularised conversational implicatures and so they might not be the best kinds of cases to focus on in exploring the kinds of inferences we make when communicating.

VIOLATING MAXIMS WITHOUT CAUSING IMPLICATURES

A central idea in Grice's approach is that we generally assume that communicators are observing the maxims. If it seems that a speaker is not observing a maxim, we look for reasons for this. Some of these reasons involve deriving implicatures so that the utterance as a whole is seen as following the maxims. While much of the discussion of Grice's ideas focuses on examples where an implicature follows from a violation of one or more maxims at the level of what is said (whether a flouting or because of a clash of maxims), it is not the case that every violation of a maxim gives rise to an implicature and neither is it that every implicature follows from the violation of a maxim. There are a number of cases, not all discussed by Grice, where a maxim is violated but that does not give rise to implicatures. We will finish this chapter by considering these cases.

'UNOSTENTATIOUS' VIOLATIONS (DECEIT OR LYING)

Grice suggested that we sometimes make what he called 'unostentatious' violations, i.e. where we violate one or more maxims without this violation being obvious to our addressees. In this case, we are likely to say that the speaker is being misleading. The most obvious cases would be straightforward lying where a speaker says something false but does not intend for the hearer to be aware of this. Suppose, for example, that Bella is mischievous or malicious and replies as follows to Adam's question about whether Calum would like some cake:

(40) I'm sure he'd love some.

If Adam has no reason to mistrust Bella, he will not realise that she is saying something false and will infer that it makes sense to offer Calum some cake. Notice, also, that even if Adam doesn't trust Bella, he will still infer that she is communicating that Calum would like some cake. So deceitful behaviour is recognised by Grice but no implicatures arise because the deceit depends on addressees not being aware of their violation.

Speakers can also be misleading by unostentatiously violating other maxims. A speaker might, for example, deliberately give less information than is required to avoid making the hearer aware of something they'd rather they didn't know.

(41) Adam: How did you get on in the exam?
       Bella: I messed up some of the questions.

If Bella messed up all of the question, then most people would agree that she is violating the maxim of quantity by not giving enough information. She does not want Adam to realise this, though, so this does not give rise to an implicature.

UNINTENDED VIOLATIONS

Another case, not much discussed by Grice, is where a communicator violates a maxim without intending to. This could be due to cultural variation with regard to how much people within a culture expect others to communicate. I might, for example, not tell you about an illness I am experiencing because I do not think it appropriate to share personal medical information. In an analysis of Mark Haddon's (2003) novel *The Curious Incident of the Dog in the Night-Time*, Semino (2014) suggests that unostentatious violations are happening when the main character, Christopher, (often) gives more information than would be expected (many readers assume that Christopher is autistic but this is not explicitly mentioned in the book). Thomas (1986, 1995) discussed this category and used the term 'infringement' to refer to it. This is an important category and very useful (e.g. for Semino's discussion just referred to), but Thomas uses the term 'infringement' differently from Grice, who used it as more or less synonymous with 'violation'. For Grice, all violations were infringements and a subset of these were unintended.

'SUSPENSION' OF MAXIMS

Some researchers also identify a category called 'suspension'. They say that maxims can be suspended in particular contexts, e.g. that there are cultures where people are not expected to say much about what they know about each other. Keenan (1976), for example, presented data showing that Malagasy speakers often provide less information about other people than they know, e.g. saying that somebody is 'either at the market or at home' when they know that they are at home. One way to deal with this is to say that the maxims are suspended here because of the cultural context. Another option, however, is to say that the maxims are operating as usual but that the context has affected what counts as 'adequate information'. An important focus of work on pragmatics has been on how communication differs in different cultural contexts.

Another case which could be considered here occurs when speakers explicitly opt out of observing a maxim. Grice gives the example of a speaker saying 'I cannot say more; my lips are sealed', and so explicitly opting out of providing enough information. This does give rise to at least one implicature, of course, since it implicates that there are reasons why the speaker does not say more.

A key thing to notice is that implicatures are not generated every time a communicator says or does something that does not follow the maxims. In order to generate implicatures, violations need to be intended and this needs to be clear to addressees.

DEVELOPING GRICE'S IDEAS

Many contemporary pragmaticists would say that Grice's most important contributions are his discussion of different kinds of meaning (and the identification of 'non-natural' meaning in particular) and the suggestion that we can work out how meanings are communicated in specific contexts with reference to rational principles.

The importance of Grice's ideas was recognised quickly and the typed-up version of his lecture on 'Logic and Conversation' was widely photocopied and shared (I first encountered Grice's ideas in this format in the 1980s). Naturally, discussion focused both on how to develop these sketchy ideas more fully and on critical consideration with a view to developing more successful approaches. The next three chapters look at approaches which developed from this critical discussion.

FINDING OUT MORE

Here are thoughts on finding out more about Grice's ideas. In my opinion, the best way to understand Grice's ideas (as with many topics) is to make mistakes in trying to apply them and then understand where you have gone wrong. This means that these exercises will work better if you have someone (e.g. a tutor) who can check your thinking and advise you. (I'm sorry I can't do that for you!)

YOUR OWN EXAMPLES

As ever, and as suggested in Chapter 1, look out for and make notes of any interesting examples you come across and see if you can suggest an account of them with reference to Grice's ideas. Here, this will usually mean deciding whether assumptions you take to be communicated are conventional implicatures, generalised conversational implicatures, or particularised conversational implicatures. If they are conventional, you will need to identify the linguistic expressions which give rise to them. For both kinds of conversational implicatures, you will need to consider how the maxims play a role in how addressees arrive at them.

QUANTITY, QUALITY, RELATION, AND MANNER

To help you understand the nature of the different maxims, try to come up with examples which violate them. Try one for each maxim and sub-maxim (so one utterance which does not give enough information, one which gives too much, one which says something false, and so on). When you do this, you should notice that it is easier for some maxims than others. Why should this be? Could it be that not all of the maxims have the same status? Asking questions like this led to the development of the approaches discussed in Chapters 3 and 4.

EXPLAINING UTTERANCES

Look at example utterances and consider:

a. What they say
b. What they implicate
c. What kind of implicature each of the ones you identify is
d. How to explain the implicature (with reference to maxims if they are conversational implicatures)

FURTHER READING

The best introductions to Grice's ideas are in introductory textbooks. Each of the textbooks listed at the end of Chapter 1 discusses Grice's ideas. Although they are not recent, Levinson (1983, Chapter 3) is still one of the best introductions and Thomas (1995, Chapter 3) is a very useful discussion with lots of good examples.

ADJUSTING THE MAXIMS
NEO-GRICEAN PRAGMATICS

All of the approaches which build on Grice have retained the idea that general principles guide pragmatic interpretation (as mentioned, production has been focused on far less often). The approaches in this chapter share with Grice the idea that the principles function like 'maxims', i.e. things which communicators aim to follow when interacting with each other. Because of this, they have been referred to as 'neo-Gricean' approaches, the idea being that they have 'renewed' Grice's ideas with some adaptations. Other approaches, including relevance theory which we discuss in the next chapter, propose something more radical in that they view pragmatic principles not as maxims but as law-like generalisations, i.e. generalisations about what we do when we interact rather than maxim-like principles which we aim to follow (and sometimes depart from for communicative reasons). Since they do not retain so much of Grice's ideas, these approaches are often termed 'post-Gricean'. One way to read this is to see them as 'only' post-Gricean without also renewing his ideas.

The most obvious property which the neo-Griceans share, apart from retaining the idea of maxim-like principles, is that they start from observations about how many maxims are necessary and what exactly they should look like. Some approaches have suggested reducing the number of principles. This follows partly from the observation that some implicatures can be equally well explained with reference to more than one maxim. Other approaches have proposed an increase in the number of principles, suggesting that we have aims in interaction not captured by Grice's maxims, such as the aim of being more or less polite, the aim of being tactful, and so on. This chapter discusses two approaches (developed by Laurence Horn and Stephen Levinson) which propose a smaller number of principles and one approach (developed by Geoffrey Leech) which proposes a greater number.

DEVELOPING GRICE'S APPROACH

Despite naming it a 'theory', Grice saw his proposal as a tentative first step towards a more fully developed account. His central insight was recognised as extremely important and there was lots of discussion of how to apply it. At the same time, there was discussion of a range of gaps and other issues. This included discussion of the details of the maxims Grice proposed and the question of whether they were all needed. Some maxims seem not to play much of a role in accounting for how we communicate and understand each other. Others seem to overlap in that it seems to be possible to use more than one of them to play the same role in explanations. The approaches discussed here arose partly from discussion of this.

QUANTITY AND RELATION: 'OVERLAPPING' MAXIMS?

In the previous chapter, I suggested that we could explain the interpretation of Bella's response in the following exchanges with reference to the first maxim of quantity, given that what Bella says each time seems not to be 'as informative as is required':

(1) Adam: What is the exam for this module like?
    Bella: Like an exam.
(2) Adam: How you getting on with your pragmatics essay?
    Bella: It's a beautiful day, isn't it? Look at that sky!

On Grice's account, since what is said is not informative enough, Adam will infer implicatures which do provide enough information.

We could equally have offered explanations for each of these which refer to the maxim of relation since they do not say something relevant (as mentioned, of course, this depends on having the fuller definition of 'relevant' which Grice knew was missing). We also looked at example (3), where the speaker says something which provides too much information. This could also be explained as a case where what is said is not relevant, since the hearer already knows it:

> (3) Adam: What is the exam for this module like?
>   Bella: It starts with all the students gathering on campus outside the exam room. Then an invigilator opens the door and invites everybody into the room...

Noticing overlaps like this led some theorists to wonder whether Grice might have suggested more maxims than we really need.

QUALITY AND MANNER: MAXIMS WHICH DON'T DO VERY MUCH

On the other hand, some maxims do not seem to be referred to very often. The most obvious examples are the maxims of quality and of manner.

While it seems reasonable to assume that communicators want their addressees to think they are being truthful (even if not fully literal), there are few cases where these maxims seem to play a role similar to other maxims, e.g. where the reasoning goes along the lines of 'the speaker would not be being truthful unless...' The one area where Grice suggested a role for the maxims of quality was in accounting for figurative language, which he suggested involved flouting of the first maxim of quality. We can illustrate this with examples (4)–(7):

> (4) Dani's tutor is a Jedi master.
> (5) You're very considerate.
> (6) That is the best idea I've ever heard.
> (7) That's not the best idea I've ever heard.

As long as it is said in our world and not in a story located in the Star Wars universe, we are likely to assume that (4) is metaphorical. Grice would say that this means the speaker has clearly violated the first maxim of quality by saying something false. The hearer will then look for an implicature the speaker could have intended and in this case decide that Dani's tutor is like a Jedi master in some ways, e.g. full of wisdom, teaching how to use powers to achieve things, etc.

In a context where the addressee has clearly not been considerate, e.g. where he has just eaten the last few of the speaker's chocolates, (5) is likely to be taken as ironic. Grice would again say that the speaker has clearly said something false and that the hearer will infer an implicature. Here, the implicature will be that the hearer is not considerate.

If we assume that the speaker in (6) really does think the idea referred to is very good, then this would count as 'hyperbole' or overstatement. Here, the false statement leads to the implicature that the idea is very good (but not literally the best the speaker has ever read).

If we assume that the speaker of (7) has a very negative attitude to the idea referred to, this would be an ironical understatement, and the implicature would be that this is far from the best idea the speaker has ever heard of.

Criticism of these ideas might seem a bit unfair, given that Grice said so little about how we might account for figurative language, but there are problems with Grice's approach here which an adequate account will need to address. Grice's approach shares properties with many traditional approaches which see metaphor as being about communicating something similar to what was said, irony as communicating 'the opposite' of what was said, and so on. What is new is that it claims to say something about what leads to interpretations of them as figurative.

One problem with this account is that it doesn't seem to be consistent with the idea that we are rational when communicating with each other. Is it rational to say something which is the opposite of what you want to communicate rather than just saying what you intend? Another is that it's not clear that all figurative language of these types involves a violation of the first maxim of quality. If (7), for example, is understood as ironical understatement, then the statement here is actually true (the speaker does think it's not the best they've ever read).

Finally, it's not clear how we work out which implicatures to draw in each case. In all four cases, Grice suggests, we recognise that the speaker has said something false and then look for another proposition which the speaker must be implicating. Looking for a related implicature is not a very clear process. What makes the hearer go for a related simile (that the tutor is like a Jedi master) in (4), the opposite of what is said (that the addressee is not very considerate) in (5), a weaker version (that this is a very good idea) in (6), and a stronger version (that it's far from the best idea) in (7).

Another problem is that the implicatures Grice suggests in each case do not seem to capture what the utterances convey. The examples in (4)–(7) do not seem to convey the same as the utterances in (8)–(11):

(8) Dani's tutor is like a Jedi master.
(9) You're not very considerate.
(10) That is a very good idea.
(11) That's far from the best idea I've ever heard of.

This is related to the problem about rationality. If the speaker intended to communicate what they could have communicated by saying the examples in (8)–(11), why not just use these utterances rather than expecting hearers to recognise a false statement and work out something different?

Overall, then, it seems that the maxim of quality is not much needed apart from in this area and even here the accounts it offers are problematic.

The maxims of manner are also not often referred to and later accounts have tended either to drop them or to subsume them in other principles. Arguably, we can find some examples where they are relevant, though.

As we saw, there are four proposed maxims of manner: avoid obscurity of expression, avoid ambiguity, be brief (I think Grice meant to be seen as playful when he added 'avoid unnecessary prolixity' in brackets after this one, making the utterance longer and more obscure than it needs to be), and be orderly. Here is a suggestion of how each could play a role.

Grice suggests that we might be obscure in order to communicate something to one person in the presence of another who we do not want to understand what we are communicating. (12) is an example we might use in the presence of a child, and the 'code-switching' (changing from English to French) in (13) might be designed to prevent people who don't speak French from understanding (the French part means 'let's not talk about it in front of the others'):

(12)   We maybe shouldn't talk about I-C-E-C-R-E-A-M
         (Adapted from Levinson 1983: 104)

(13)   Given what we know about the situation, *ne parlons pas devant les autres.*

Both of these utterances are risky, of course. First, the child who hears (12) might be able to spell, and the others who hear (13) might understand French. Second, whether or not the other people who hear can understand, it is very likely that saying something in a way which excludes some people who hear you will be seen as rude (we consider impoliteness in Chapter 5).

When considering 'ambiguity', it is important to notice that Grice did not mean the term in the sense in which it is usually understood in linguistics today, i.e. to refer to expressions which have more than one linguistic meaning (there are so many of these that it would be very hard to avoid using them). Rather, he meant cases where it is not possible to understand in a specific context what meaning is intended. Grice gives an example from poetry where, of course, deliberate ambiguity is common, and another example involving a complex play on words:

(14)   Never seek to tell thy love
         Love that never told can be

(15)   *Peccavi*

(14), from a poem by William Blake, is ambiguous in more than one way. The word *love* can refer to an emotion or a person who is loved while *tell* and *told* (different forms of the same lexical item, of course) have senses about counting something as well as speaking about something. The second line could be about a love which cannot be spoken about or counted or about a love that cannot exist if spoken about or counted. There are also other ways of reading the lines. Grice suggests that we are likely to entertain the different readings rather than choosing one partly because of what we know about 'the sophistication of the poet' (itself open to more than one reading by the way) and partly because the poem keeps the different readings active by how it develops. We could also say that this is because of things we expect from poetry and possible experience of developing literary interpretations.

(14) involves readings which Grice saw as fairly equal in straightforwardness, sophistication, and so on. (15) involves one reading that is

more straightforward than the other. This utterance of the Latin *peccavi* appeared in a telegram from a general who had just captured the town of Sind. This would usually be translated into English as 'I have sinned'. As Grice says, the ambiguity here is about sound (*I have sinned* and *I have Sind* sound identical in spoken English) and the reader of the telegram is expected to recognise and to see that the general has gone a very round-about way to communicate that he has captured the town. It would seem, therefore, that this example could be explained as a flouting of the maxim 'avoid obscurity of expression' rather than 'avoid ambiguity'.

It is worth asking whether cases like these really fit with Grice's account in general. Are these cases where the maxim is flouted and so hearers need to look for an implicature to justify their assumption that the maxims are being observed? It might be possible to develop such an account but these effects seem to be more to do with more than one sense being salient and both seeming appropriate in the context.

It is fairly easy to think of examples where a speaker is less brief than would usually be expected. Grice's example is not the most natural one (I've adapted it here):

(16) She produced a series of notes that corresponded to the score of the song 'Let It Go'.

Grice suggests that if we came across this in the review of a performance, we would wonder why the reviewer hadn't written something more simple, e.g.:

(17) She sang 'Let It Go'.

Hearing (16), we would be likely to assume that there was something wrong with the performance.

Arguably, examples like these could be explained with reference to another maxim, e.g. we could refer to the maxim of quantity and say that the reviewer has given us more information than we need. On the other hand, the account in terms of (non-)brevity works, and the ideas in some more recent theories could be seen as building on this idea.

The maxim which says to 'be orderly' has been used in cases such as the following:

(18) She sang 'Let It Go' and left the stage.

Here we assume that the singer first sang the song and then left the stage. We assume this because we assume that the speaker is presenting events in the order in which they occurred. We would assume something different if we reversed the conjuncts:

(19) She left the stage and sang 'Let It Go'.

Here we are likely to assume that the singer left the stage before singing the song, which is unusual. We could say that the assumption about the sequence of events is a 'generalised conversational implicature' where we make an inference based on general assumptions about the world. If the singer left the stage before singing the song, we need to say so, either by saying (19) or maybe by cancelling the implicature explicitly as:

(20) She sang 'Let It Go' and left the stage, but not in that order.

The fact that we can cancel the assumption would count, for Grice, as evidence that this is indeed a conversational implicature.

It seems hard to find cases of 'flouting' this maxim, i.e. cases where the speaker seems to be blatantly violating the maxim in order to implicate something. We might argue that this could occur in literary contexts but it would require specific situations which cannot occur in a reverse order, e.g. 'I've been alive for a while and now I'm waiting to be born' but an utterance like this is more likely to encourage us to think of the term *born* metaphorically as in the following line from a song by Bob Dylan:

(21) He not busy being born is busy dying.
      (Bob Dylan *It's Alright Ma (I'm only bleeding)*)

Overall, then, there seem to be some cases where the maxims of quality and manner could be used but they do not seem as central to pragmatics as the maxims of quantity and relation. Following this line of reasoning, the two approaches we are about to look at aimed to develop a more economical account with fewer assumed pragmatic principles.

HORN'S TWO PRINCIPLES

Horn and Levinson both responded to Grice's ideas by focusing on questions about the details of the maxims and their relationship. They noticed that, as we have seen, some maxims seem not to be much needed while others seem to overlap, in that some examples could be equally well explained by reference to different maxims.

Horn's response was to propose just two principles which he saw as relating to more than two of Grice's maxims. These are a 'Q' or 'Quantity' Principle and an 'R' or 'Relation' Principle. Roughly, the Q Principle says that we should give as much information as is needed while the R Principle says we should not say more than is needed:

Horn's Pragmatic Principles:

> *Q Principle*:
> Make your contribution sufficient;
> Say as much as you can (given R)
> *R Principle*:
> Make your contribution necessary;
> Say no more than you must (given Q)

It probably occurs to you straight away that these principles seem to contradict each other or at least to push in opposite directions. This is intentional. Horn's idea is that one principle pushes you to make sure you say everything you can while the other pushes you to say no more than you need to. Your utterance will then strike a balance between the two. You might also think that they seem to be close to Grice's two maxims of quantity, since they seem to be saying something like that what you say should be 'as informative as is required' and not 'more informative than is required' (the phrases used in these two maxims). This is also intentional as Horn sees the Q Principle as similar to the first maxim of quantity and the R Principle as similar to the second maxim of quantity. However, he also sees the Q Principle as subsuming two of the maxims of manner ('avoid obscurity' and 'avoid ambiguity') and the R Principle as subsuming the maxim of relation ('be relevant') and one of the maxims of manner ('be brief'). As mentioned in the last chapter, Gricean analyses often seem to be equally plausibly given by referring to the maxim of quantity or the maxim of relation. At the same time, Grice was not sure how to define 'relevant'. Horn's proposal solves these two issues at once.

Overall, Horn claims that his framework is both simpler and more coherent than Grice's account. He sees communication as constrained by the interaction of a requirement to give enough information and a requirement not to give too much information. We can see one of these principles as focusing on what works for hearers (who need to receive enough information and not be left wondering about exactly what's intended) and the other as focusing on what works for speakers (who don't want to put more effort into what they say than they need to).

Horn connects his ideas with those of other thinkers including George Kingsley Zipf who, among other things, proposed a Principle of Least Effort (Zipf 1949) and suggested that, when considering verbal communication, this can be understood as involving a principle of speaker economy and a principle of hearer economy. These are in conflict since fully following a principle of speaker economy would lead to speakers making minimal contributions, leaving hearers to work out meanings, while a principle of hearer economy would involve spelling things out very fully so that hearers have very little to do in order to understand (putting aside for now that processing longer linguistic stimuli takes more effort than processing shorter ones). The Q Principle is hearer focused, pushing speakers to provide enough information for hearers (given the R Principle). The R Principle is speaker focused, pushing speakers towards saying as little as possible (given the Q Principle).

The key question, of course, is about how Horn's approach explains the pragmatics of verbal communication. There are some cases which seem to be explainable with reference to just one of the principles. Here are two examples we can use to show this:

(22) Some of the students seemed to enjoy your class.
(23) Can you pass the salt?

In many contexts, (22) would be taken to implicate that not all of the students seemed to enjoy the class. We can explain this by referring to the Q Principle. If all of the students seemed to enjoy it, then it follows from the Q Principle ('say as much as you can') that the speaker should say so. Given that they haven't said this, then either they must think that not all of the students seemed to enjoy it or that they don't know whether they all did.

In many contexts (in fact, so many that many theorists now think this has become a conventionalised, maybe even linguistic, meaning), (23) would be taken as a request to pass the salt. If there is no reason to doubt whether the hearer is able to pass the salt, then this cannot be all that the speaker intends. Horn uses the term 'license' here, saying that this utterance 'licenses' the hearer to assume that the speaker intended more, i.e. that the speaker would like the hearer to pass them the salt. Why does the speaker not ask directly? Because the R Principle says that we should say no more than is necessary. If the hearer can infer the request without it being spelled out, there is no need to say it explicitly. In Chapter 5, we will see how implicatures such as this can be related to ideas about (im)politeness.

For some utterances, we can refer to both the Q and the R Principles. Consider again this exchange:

(24) Adam: Do you think Calum would like a piece of this cake?
       Bella: He's vegan.

Adam assumes that Bella has made her contribution sufficient (saying as much as she can given the Q Principle) and necessary (saying no more than she needs to given the R Principle). A common assumption is that someone who is vegan avoids eating or using things which contain animal products. Knowing this, Bella does not need to say more than that Calum is vegan for Adam to infer that he won't want cake. On the other hand, if Calum's being vegan was not going to affect the likelihood of his eating the cake then, given the Q Principle, Bella should have made clear that his being vegan doesn't affect the question of whether he might like some cake. Therefore, Bella must be intending to implicate that Calum will not want any cake because he's vegan. Notice that both principles play a role here and that there is not a problem in integrating them even though they push in different directions.

SCALAR IMPLICATURES

One of the most influential aspects of Horn's approach is his work on what have been termed 'scalar implicatures', which (22) can be used to illustrate. Horn points out that some expressions have a logical relationship to each other which relates to their semantic 'strength'.

The expressions *some* and *all* are in this relationship (strictly speaking, of course, this is about what the words mean rather than just the words themselves). *All* is stronger than *some* in that *all X* 'entails' *some X* (if we attribute a property to all of a certain group X, then we must think that the property is attributable to some of the group X). Given pragmatic principles (the Q Principle, on Horn's approach) using a semantically weaker expression usually implicates the negation of a stronger one. So, for example, when you say that some of the students seemed to enjoy my class then you implicate that not all of them seemed to.

Here are some other examples of expressions which form scales (sometimes termed 'Horn scales', recognising Horn's work in identifying them):

Some 'Horn Scales':

some	*all*	
possible/ly	*probable/ly*	*certain/ly*
warm	*hot*	
like	*love*	
or	*and*	

As we said, if you say that some X have a property then you implicate that not all X have that property. If you say something is possible, you implicate that is it not probable. And so on.

We can see that these are implicatures because they can be contextually or explicitly cancelled as in these examples:

(25) If you are under 25 or a full-time student, you are entitled to a discount.

(26) Calum likes Dani. I don't know whether he loves her, though.

It might not be obvious straight away but it seems that *or* and *and* form a scale. If I say that we are having pasta bake or stir-fry for supper, you are likely to infer that we will not be having both. However, contextual assumptions about how discounts work mean that we don't infer 'not *and*' when we hear or read (25), i.e. we think that someone who is both a student and under 25 will be entitled to a discount.

In (26), we might assume that Calum doesn't love Dani based on the first part of the utterance, given the use of *likes* rather than *loves*, but the speaker goes on to cancel this explicitly and this won't seem odd for most hearers.

Horn's ideas on 'scalar implicatures' have been very influential, and there has been a lot of discussion on exactly how they work. One question is about their exact status and how they arise. Another is about why and how they are sometimes not inferred. Scalar implicatures have been the focus of much experimental work to investigate these questions. Noveck (2018) and Noveck and Sperber (2004) are useful introductions to work on experimental pragmatics.

LEVINSON'S THREE PRINCIPLES

Levinson's development of Grice's work is similar to Horn's in that he proposes to reduce the number of principles while retaining the idea that they are maxim-like principles which people aim to follow in verbal interactions. Like Horn, Levinson noticed that some of Grice's maxims, and some examples, seem to point in different directions. Some lead to the implicature of something stronger than what was said and some to the negation of something that was not said. Here are adapted versions of two of Levinson's examples:

(27) He turned the key and the engine started.
(28) Some of the workers voted to accept the pay offer.

(27) is likely to be taken to implicate that the engine started as a direct result of the turning of the key (which we infer is the car's ignition key). So here we assume something that hasn't been said. (28) is likely to be taken to implicate that not all of the workers voted to accept the pay offer. So here we assume that something not said is not intended.

Like Horn, Levinson goes on to propose a smaller number of pragmatic principles. He proposes three principles, each of which has associated heuristics for speakers and hearer. Here is one way of summarising them, with a speaker's maxim and a hearer's 'corollary' (which we can think of as a heuristic related to the speaker's maxim) for each one:

Levinson's Pragmatic Principles:

> *Q-Principle*:
> Speaker's maxim:
> Don't say less than is required (bearing the I-Principle in mind)
> Hearer's corollary:
> 'What isn't said isn't'
> *I-Principle*:
> Speaker's maxim:
> Don't say more than is required (bearing the Q-Principle in mind)
> Hearer's corollary:
> 'What is expressed simply is stereotypically exemplified'
> *M-Principle*:
> Speaker's maxim:
> Don't use a marked expression without a reason
> Hearer's corollary:
> 'What's said in an abnormal way isn't normal'

Levinson sees his Q-Principle as corresponding to Grice's first maxim of quantity, which says to be 'as informative as is required', the I-Principle as corresponding to the second maxim of quantity, which says not to be 'more informative than required', and the M-Principle as corresponding to three of the maxims of manner: 'be brief', 'avoid obscurity', and 'avoid ambiguity'. You will have noticed that Levinson's first two principles are similar to Horn's two principles.

Here are three examples to illustrate how these principles work:

(29) It'll take us over an hour to get there.
(30) I took a corner too quickly and fell off my bike.
(31) I went into the exam room and sat there for three hours putting words onto the answer sheet with a pen.

In (29), we are likely to assume that it will not take us two hours or longer to get there (which would still be over one hour, of course), since the speaker would not be giving enough information if so and we can assume that 'what isn't said isn't'. In (30), we can assume that the speaker fell off their bike as a result of taking the corner too quickly, since this sequence of events is 'stereotypical' in the sense that we have knowledge of things like this happening and we can expect the speaker not to have said what they don't need to say, i.e. because they trust us to work it out from our world knowledge (this is 'expressed simply' so we can assume that it is 'stereotypically exemplified'). In (31), the marked/'abnormal' expression (*putting words onto the answer sheet with a pen*) suggests that there is something marked or unusual about what happened. Otherwise, the speaker would have used an unmarked expression like *I spent three hours on the exam*. We are likely to derive an implicature that the speaker did not do a good job of answering the questions.

PRAGMATIC 'INTRUSION' (PRAGMATICS AND WHAT IS SAID)

Levinson's approach has more to say about the pragmatics of what is said or directly communicated than Horn's, and he proposes to apply his pragmatic principles in explaining this. Levinson focuses closely on Grice's notion of 'generalised conversational implicature' and he develops a much more detailed account than Grice of how these implicatures are inferred, noting that some of them are about 'what is said' and so not really implicatures, e.g. inferences about the referent of *a finger* in 'I broke a finger yesterday'. Levinson (and some other pragmaticists) suggests that this is better treated as an aspect of what is directly communicated ('what is said' for Grice) rather than as an independent implicature.

A large amount of empirical work, particularly experimental work, has focused on what evidence can help us to choose between accounts which assume something like 'generalised conversational implicatures', often referred to now with the more general term 'default inferences', and those which do not.

LEECH'S APPROACH

The final approach considered in this chapter was developed by Geoffrey Leech (Leech 1983, 2014). Leech made a number of significant contributions to pragmatics including on how utterances can be more or less polite (which I discuss in Chapter 5). He also asked the question of how many principles and maxims we need in order to explain communication and came up with a different answer to that of

Horn and Levinson. Rather than suggesting a reduction in the number of maxims required, Leech suggested that we need more.

Leech took seriously Grice's idea that we can explain utterance interpretation in context by assuming that we aim to follow maxim-like principles when communicating. Rather than focusing simply on the maxims Grice proposed and questions about these and their interaction, Leech asked whether there might be other maxims which we aim to follow and concluded that there are. In particular, he suggested that there are a number of maxims which play a role in how we assess the politeness of particular communicative acts. He suggested that these fall under an overarching Politeness Principle which operated alongside Grice's Cooperative Principle. Leech began working on this in the 1970s (Leech 1977) and published a book on politeness in 1983. He returned to this topic in 2014. Here is his politeness principle as stated there:

(32) Principle of Politeness:
      In order to be polite, S[elf] expresses or implies meanings that associate a favourable value with what pertains to O[ther] or associate an unfavourable value with what pertains to S[elf]
      (Leech 2014: 90)

Leech saw this as an additional principle to the Cooperative Principle proposed by Grice. In fact, he saw it as 'preliminary' in that communication depends on the individuals involved being polite to each other. If we are not polite to each other, Leech suggested, communication breaks down and the Cooperative Principle does not apply.

Leech proposed a number of maxims which fall under the Principle of Politeness. The principles all have to do with acting positively towards others and negatively towards yourself. In his 2014 book, these are:

Maxims of Politeness:

> *Generosity*:
> Give a high value to O[ther]'s wants.
> *Tact*:
> Give a low value to S[elf]'s wants.
> *Approbation*:
> Give a high value to O's qualities.

Modesty:
Give a low value to S's qualities.
Obligation of S to O:
Give a high value to S's obligation to O.
Obligation of O to S:
Give a low value to O's obligation to S.
Agreement:
Give a high value to O's opinions.
Opinion reticence:
Give a low value to S's opinions.
Sympathy:
Give a high value to O's feelings.
Feeling reticence:
Give a low value to S's feelings.

(adapted from Leech 2014: 91)

The overarching principle can be seen as having a positive and a negative aspect since it is about acting both positively towards others and negatively towards yourself. Each of the maxims is expressed in such a way as to do one or the other of these. The list above is made up of pairs where the first of each is about acting positively towards others and the second is about acting negatively towards yourself.

'MODIFIED OCCAM'S RAZOR'

So Leech is suggesting increasing the number of maxims and is open to the possibility that there could be even more. In fact, his 2014 book proposes more than were present in his 1983 book.

Many theorists have seen what they think of as a proliferation of maxims as a mistake. This relates to a general methodological aim in much scientific work, including in pragmatics, to aim for theories which are as simple as possible. In philosophy and science in general, the principle known as 'Occam's razor', attributed to William of Occam (also spelled Ockham or Ocham), a Franciscan friar who lived from 1287 to 1347, says (in one translation) that 'entities should not be multiplied without necessity'. This is usually taken to mean that we should not assume anything more than we need to in reasoning, problem-solving, and scientific theorising (among other things). In fact, Grice (1978: 118–119) proposed a 'modified Occam's razor' which says that 'senses are not to be multiplied beyond necessity'.

Grice's modified Occam's razor is about linguistic meaning. The idea is that we shouldn't assume a word has two linguistic meanings unless we have to. Let's start with a clear case of ambiguity:

(33) a. We went for a walk on the shore yesterday. There was a seal splashing and barking in the water right next to us.
      b. There's a puddle beside the shower door. I think the seal's gone.

Clearly, these two senses of *seal* (there are others, of course) are not related. It's just a coincidence of English that the word for these two things is pronounced in the same way (and has the same spelling). In fact, we also assume that the two words have different origins (one has Germanic origins and the other comes from Latin).

Now consider (34):

(34) There's a draught from that window. We need to fix the seal.

Here, we can assume that *seal* has the same meaning as in (33b) and that we work out in context what kind of seal the speaker has in mind (the kind you get in windows rather than the one you get in shower doors).

Any account would have to accept that there are two senses involved in (33) but it's natural to treat the senses in (33b) and (34) as the same. Rather than suggesting a different sense for each place in a building where we expect to find something to complete a closure, we assume one meaning which is understood in different ways in different contexts.

Grice's modified Occam's razor supports an account in terms of pragmatic principles for what had been thought of previously as cases of linguistic ambiguity. In fact, one of Grice's key aims in developing his approach was to show that natural languages are far less ambiguous than had previously been assumed. We can illustrate by looking at examples containing *and*:

(35) Adam is from London and Bella is from Aberdeen.
(36) He brushed his teeth and went to bed.
(37) She forgot to water the plant and it died.

The closest term to *and* in logical languages is the connective &, which simply conjoins two propositions. Roughly, we can say that the meaning of *P* & *Q* is simply that *P* is true and *Q* is true. It seems that (35) simply states two separate facts (it tells us where Adam is from and also where Bella is from) but when we hear (36) and (37) we assume something different. In (36), we are likely to think that the brushing of teeth happened before he went to bed and when we hear (37) we are likely to think that the plant died because she forgot to water it. With the logical expression &, the order of the conjuncts doesn't matter so that *P* & *Q* means the same as *Q* & *P*. This seems to work for utterances like (35) but not for (36) and (37). If we swap the order of conjuncts in (35) as in (38), the utterance seems to mean much the same thing:

(38)   Bella is from Aberdeen and Adam is from London.

By contrast, reversing the order of the conjuncts in (36) and (37), as in (39) and (40), makes them mean different things:

(39)   He went to bed and brushed his teeth.
(40)   The plant died and she forgot to water it.

In (39), we are likely to think that he went to bed before he brushed his teeth rather than the other way round. In (40), the consequential or causal relationship disappears and we are not likely to make specific assumptions about the ordering of the events.

One way to respond to data like this is to say that natural languages contain lots of ambiguous expressions, *and* being one of them. Grice's ideas make it possible to see *and* as having one meaning, the same as logical &, and to see the differences as arising because of implicatures inferred by hearers. This seems plausible because the assumptions about ordering and causation can be cancelled explicitly or contextually. You can, for example, add some words to cancel these implicatures:

(41)   He brushed his teeth and went to bed but not in that order.
(42)   She forgot to water the plant and it died but it would have died anyway so it wasn't her fault.

Support for a pragmatic approach also comes from the fact that words in other languages which correspond to *and* give rise to the same kinds of interpretations and that there are even more ways in which we can see conjuncts as connected, as illustrated by (43) and (44):

(43) He got into the bath and read a chapter of his book.
(44) She took a deep breath, ran to the edge of the diving board, and jumped.

In (43) we assume not only that reading the book chapter happened after he got into the bath but also that he read it while he was in the bath. In (44) we assume not only that she jumped after she ran but also that she jumped off of the diving board and into a pool.

Given the general aim to keep theories simple, and the specific aims of pragmaticists to assume as little ambiguity and as simple pragmatic theories as possible, it's not surprising that Leech's proposal of more maxims did not seem like a good idea to many pragmaticists. Nevertheless, it is always possible that things are not as simple as they could possibly be and so we might indeed need to propose more theoretical ideas in some cases. Just as some terms are ambiguous and so we cannot make the simplest possible suggestion for what they mean linguistically, so we might need to assume more principles to account for specific pragmatic phenomena. One question about Leech's approach is whether each of his maxims is actually a maxim of the type suggested by Grice or simply a statement of more general cultural assumptions which are part of the context affecting interpretations.

PRAGMALINGUISTICS AND SOCIOPRAGMATICS

Another important contribution made by Leech, and developed by his student Jenny Thomas (1983), was to distinguish 'general pragmatics' from 'pragmalinguistics' and 'sociopragmatics', as represented in Figure 3.1.

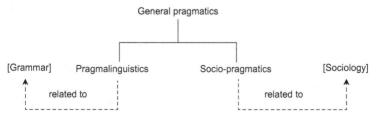

FIGURE 3.1 Leech's categories of pragmatics (based on Leech 1983: 11)

The idea here was to separate general pragmatics, which Leech described as 'fairly abstract' from 'language-specific' studies (pragmalinguistics) and 'culture-specific' studies (sociopragmatics). These are three separate things and not, as the diagram might seem to suggest, arranged hierarchically (general pragmatics is distinct from the other two rather than encompassing them). Leech, then, was not assuming that pragmatic principles are wholly universal but recognising that there are some details which are different in different cultural contexts. By contrast, many approaches which developed from Grice's ideas assumed that pragmatic principles are wholly universal.

While not all of Leech's specific proposals have been adopted by later pragmaticists, his work on pragmatics in general and politeness in particular has been influential. We look at a range of ideas which have been proposed to account for what makes utterances more or less polite or impolite in Chapter 5.

FINDING OUT MORE

Here are some ideas for things you might do to develop understanding of ideas in the chapter and to find out more, followed by some suggested further reading.

YOUR OWN EXAMPLES

As ever, it's always a good idea to notice and try to explain your own examples. Look out for and make notes of any interesting examples you come across and see if you can suggest an account of them with reference to the ideas in this chapter. For this chapter, this will mean referring to the principles proposed by Horn, Levinson, or Leech. One thing to consider is how we can decide whether something not said should be taken as communicated (because there was no need to say it) or whether its negation is being communicated (because it would have been said if it was the case).

COMPARING APPROACHES

Another useful exercise is to compare how different approaches would account for particular examples. You might, for example, look at examples you have discussed before and consider how different approaches would account for them. You could do this with examples you looked at after reading previous chapters or new ones you have identified now. You might also look at examples discussed in this chapter.

SOME MORE SPECIFIC QUESTIONS

It's important to think critically when developing and evaluating pragmatic theories. This is, of course, how theories develop, as critical discussion of an approach can lead to new developments (as we have discussed here). In considering the approaches discussed here (and other approaches), consider whether there are gaps in the explanation. How exactly, for example, do hearers know which principle, or combination of principles, to refer to when explaining a particular interpretation? How do we know when to assume that something *is* the case when it hasn't been said (e.g. assuming that taking a corner too quickly caused somebody to fall off their bike) and when to assume something not said *is not* the case (e.g. assuming that not all of the students enjoyed my class when somebody says that some of them did)?

FURTHER READING

The textbooks listed at the end of chapter one contain useful discussion of these ideas. Here are discussions by Horn, Leech and Levinson themselves:

1. Horn, Laurence R. 1988. Pragmatic theory. In F. Newmeyer (ed.) *Linguistics: The Cambridge Survey. Volume 1: Linguistic Theory: Foundations*. Cambridge University Press: 113–145.
2. Leech, Geoffrey N. 1983. *Principles of Pragmatics*. Longman.
3. Leech, Geoffrey. 2014. *Principles of Politeness*. Oxford University Press.
4. Levinson, Stephen C. 2000. *Presumptive Meanings: The Theory of Generalised Conversational Implicature*. MIT Press.

4

PRINCIPLES AND HEURISTICS
RELEVANCE THEORY

The previous chapter focused on 'neo-Gricean' pragmatic theories which suggest different numbers of maxim-like pragmatic principles. This chapter looks at a different approach, relevance theory, which suggests principles understood not as maxim-like but as generalisations about cognition and communication. These principles are not seen as things we aim to follow but as generalisations about what we actually do. The principles refer to a technical definition of 'relevance' which developed from discussion of Grice's ideas.

A GENERALISATION ABOUT COMMUNICATION

Don't pay any attention to this sentence; it's not relevant to you.

I assume that you have not followed the instruction you have just read. It would be odd if you did, given that you are reading a book which explicitly claims to contain things that are relevant to you (if you're interested in pragmatics). More generally, whenever somebody makes clear to somebody else that they are intentionally communicating with them, this creates the expectation that the communicator must have in mind an interpretation which will justify the effort involved in arriving at that interpretation. This is the central idea behind relevance theory.

Consider two ways in which somebody might act as they move aside when you and they are walking towards each other in the street. First, imagine they move aside to let you pass without particularly looking at you. You are unlikely to think about them much and will probably carry on walking much as you were doing before. Now imagine that they make eye contact with you, raise their head, gesture behind themself with it, and then move aside. You might now think that they are trying to communicate something to you. How will you behave differently when this happens? Relevance theory predicts that you will put more effort into looking for something that the other person is trying to communicate. You are likely to look more carefully to see what they might be trying to draw your attention to.

This might seem very simple. If someone is communicating with you, you'll try to work out what they're communicating. The claim is, though, that the expectations raised when you recognise somebody is trying to communicate are fairly precise and precise enough to explain how we understand each other when communicating. To understand how this works, we first need to look at how relevance theory defines the notion of 'relevance'.

DEFINING RELEVANCE: EFFECTS AND EFFORT

As mentioned above, one area where Grice knew he had not been explicit enough was in his proposal of a maxim of 'relation' which simply says 'be relevant'. Grice said:

> Though the maxim itself is terse, its formulation conceals a number of problems that exercise me a good deal: questions about what different kinds and focuses of relevance there may be, how these shift in the course of a talk exchange, how to allow for the fact that subjects of conversation are legitimately changed, and so on. I find the treatment of such questions exceedingly difficult, and I hope to revert to them in a later work.
>
> *(Grice 1975: 46)*

Grice never did return to this fully. In developing relevance theory, Dan Sperber and Deirdre Wilson considered how the notion of 'relevance' could be defined more technically and proposed that this could be understood as being about the effects we can derive from something and the effort we put in to getting them. They noticed that we have intuitions about the effects we can derive from something and about how much effort is involved in deriving them and that these seem to connect with ideas about how worthwhile it is to interpret an utterance.

Let's consider effects first. Would the following utterance seem worth hearing if somebody said it to you now?

(1) The temperature's going to drop to below zero tomorrow.

Assuming that you are not in a location where the temperature is often around zero (I'm assuming this is degrees Celsius), or already is, I think you would say this passes on some useful information. I am typing this in a city where the temperature is currently 12 degrees and I am assuming it will be similar tomorrow. If it's going to be below zero, I will wear different clothes and might not cycle to work (since freezing road surfaces can be slippery).

Now consider the following utterance and consider whether it seems more or less significant than (1):

(2) The temperature's going to drop to minus fifteen tomorrow.

My guess is that this seems more significant since minus fifteen is far colder than zero degrees. It's also far colder than I ever expect it to be here. (2) contradicts a number of assumptions I have at the moment and gives rise to more implications than (1). I will have to rethink my wardrobe and my behaviour more than I would have done for (1).

This kind of thinking leads to the first part of Sperber and Wilson's definition of relevance, which says that the more effects something has, the more relevant it is. We can get further evidence for this by considering (3):

(3) The temperature was below zero in Inverness on the 10th of March 1846.

I expect that this seems less significant (or 'relevant') than (1) and that you are even likely to say that nothing interesting follows from it (unless you have a reason to be interested in the temperature in Inverness on or around the 10th of March in 1846). So relevance theory assumes that something is 'relevant' to the extent that it gives rise to effects and that the more effects it gives rise to the more relevant it is.

Now consider (4):

(4) The temperature's going to drop below zero tomorrow and sixteen times sixteen is two hundred and fifty six.

Does this seem more or less relevant than (1)? I expect you to say that it seems less relevant. This seems to be because nothing significant follows from the statement of the arithmetical calculation in the second clause. It adds processing effort but does not lead to any more effects.

The second part of the definition suggested by Sperber and Wilson focuses on effort. The idea here is that the more effort involved in processing something, the less relevant it is. Consider these two possible answers to the question of how much something costs:

(5) Fifteen pounds.
(6) One pound more than eight pounds plus six pounds.

Here, I expect (6) to seem less relevant than (5) and this is because of the extra effort involved in understanding the price being communicated which does not lead to any obvious effects.

Putting these ideas together, we can come up with a comparative definition of relevance as follows (this is a simplified version of Sperber and Wilson's definition):

Comparative definition of 'relevance':
a. The more effects something has, the more relevant it is.
b. The more effort involved in interpreting something, the less relevant it is.

Relevance theory assumes three kinds of effect: strengthening existing assumptions, contradicting existing assumptions, and contextual implication, which involves inferring something new from the combination of contextual assumptions and new information.

I have illustrated this so far with examples of verbal communication. However, this definition of relevance can be applied in thinking about anything we can pay attention to, whether it involves communication or not.

Suppose, for example, that as I type this I think I hear a car crash outside. I then rush outside and see that a car has indeed crashed into another car in the street. This strengthens my initial assumption that a car has crashed.

Seeing that a car has crashed also has contextual implications for me. Given what I know about car crashes, I will infer that people might be injured, that people are likely to be upset or in shock, that the car owners will have large bills or insurance claims to deal with, and so on.

Finally, suppose that I rush outside and see no signs of a car crash. Maybe I see a rubbish truck and decide that the noise I heard was made by bins being hoisted and emptied into the truck. This would then contradict my assumption that a car crash had happened.

The more effects like these something has, the more relevant it is. The more effort involved in deriving these effects, the less relevant it is.

TWO PRINCIPLES AND A HEURISTIC

The next step in understanding the theory is to see how this notion plays a role in communication and, before that, in cognition in general.

The claim that relevance theory makes about cognition is that our minds in general are on the lookout for as many effects as possible for as little effort as possible. This is formulated in relevance theory as aiming to 'maximise' relevance and is described in what is now termed the 'Cognitive Principle of Relevance':

Cognitive Principle of Relevance:

Human cognition is geared towards the maximisation of relevance.

What does this mean? It means that, in general, we are looking to derive as many effects as we can and to expend as little effort as possible in deriving them. As we go about our lives, our minds look to notice things that are relevant in that they give rise to effects. We look for as many of these as we can and we aim not to spend too much effort looking for them.

I am sitting on a train as I type this. As I walked into the station on my way to catch the train, there were lots of things I could have paid attention to. I noticed a puddle on the ground outside the station and moved around it. The puddle was worth noticing as there was a contextual implication that my shoe would get wet if I didn't avoid it. As I entered the station, I walked past lots of other people. I noticed where they were and how they were moving and changed my direction to avoid people I might otherwise bump into. My mind in general was looking for effects. I had no special expectations but I was aware of the kinds of things to notice on a typical day. At the same time, I didn't waste effort by searching further for these effects. I didn't, for example, look closely at everybody I saw in case I had met any of them before and maybe didn't recognise them. I didn't study each part of the ground carefully in case there was liquid or objects there that I might not want to step on. Overall, the cognitive principle of relevance says that our minds work in such a way as to get as many effects as possible for as little effort as possible.

RELEVANCE AND COMMUNICATION

The communicative principle of relevance aims to capture the insight which I discussed at the start of this chapter, which is that when we notice that people intend to communicate with us, this gives rise to specific expectations of relevance. Briefly, we assume that the communicator believes that we can come up with an interpretation of what they are communicating which will be relevant enough, i.e. provide enough effects to be worth the effort involved in arriving at them.

Suppose that somebody I was about to walk past as I headed into the station this morning held a hand up in front of me. I would recognise that they intend to communicate with me and wonder what they are trying to communicate. I would now have an expectation that there are effects which they intend me to recover as a result of interpreting their behaviour. Suppose they then turn their head towards the ground where I am about to step. I will now expect to find something significant when I look there. I might then notice something hazardous, e.g. some messy spilled food, which I might not otherwise have noticed. Recognising their intention to communicate would have given rise to expectations of relevance and led me to expend more effort looking for effects than I would have done if they hadn't communicated with me. This idea is expressed in the 'Communicative Principle of Relevance'.

Communicative Principle of Relevance:

Every ostensive stimulus conveys a presumption of its own optimal relevance.

This is less clear on its own than the Cognitive Principle because understanding it requires understanding what an 'ostensive stimulus' is and what 'optimal' relevance means.

Put simply, an ostensive stimulus is one which draws attention to itself, making clear that it is intended to be understood as communicating something. This book and all the parts which it is made up of are ostensive stimuli, as is the gesture made by the person I have just described holding up a hand towards me. As I entered the station I saw other ostensive stimuli, e.g. adverts and television news playing on a big screen in the station. The main one I was interested in was the notice board which said which platform my train would be leaving on and whether it was on time.

The relevance-theoretic notion of ostensive communication develops from Grice's ideas about meaning. Grice's notion of 'non-natural meaning' or 'meaning$_{NN}$' referred to cases where a meaning is understood because of a recognition that it is intended. It's not enough simply for somebody to intend somebody else to understand something. I can, for example, move a chair in a restaurant so that people who work there can see some spilled food, intending them to see the food and clean it up without intending to communicate this to them. If, however, I say to a member of staff that 'there's some food spilled under the chair', then I am both intentionally communicating with them and they need to recognise that my utterance is intentionally communicative in order to understand me. When we recognise an intention to communicate and that intention plays a role in us understanding what is communicated, we have an example of what Grice called non-natural meaning. It is cases of non-natural meaning which fall within the scope of Grice's Cooperative Principle and the maxims which it subsumes.

Sperber and Wilson's notion of ostensive communication is not identical to Grice's non-natural meaning but the key thing for relevance theory is that some behaviour makes manifest an intention to communicate and this activates the Communicative Principle of Relevance and makes us expect to find something the communicator could have intended which has enough effects to justify the effort involved in looking for them.

ABILITIES AND PREFERENCES

Another idea in relevance theory is that what a communicator intends has to be consistent with their abilities and preferences, i.e. what they intend is limited by what they are able to communicate and what they prefer to communicate (or not).

Suppose that the stranger draws my attention to spilled food on the ground and I notice that it is what remains of a meal from a takeaway near the station which my friend owns. I might be amused to see that the food came from there and I might think about what my friend would make of this but the stranger cannot be intending to communicate this because they can't know about my friend and the restaurant.

Preferences are relevant in more than one way. They might be relevant when somebody says something that could be taken as rude. Suppose I serve my friend a plate of food and they ask me:

(7) What kind of food is this?

I could decide that my friend doesn't like the look of the food and that this is a rude rhetorical question. If this occurs to me, though, I might decide that they wouldn't be so rude intentionally and so decide that they must simply be curious about the dish. Sometimes jokes play on uncertainties about things like this, e.g. if I ask a guest in my house when they will be leaving, they might joke about me acting as if I want them to leave as quickly as possible.

We might also explain some formulations with reference to preferences, e.g. the use of polite euphemistic expressions or marked forms such as using *elderly* rather than *old* or *not the brightest student* rather than something more negative.

There is one more important thing to add to the picture, which is to say what people actually do when interpreting a communicative act. To explain this, relevance theory proposes that interpretation involves a heuristic which follows from the above assumptions. Here it is:

Relevance-Guided Comprehension Heuristic:

Follow a path of least effort in computing cognitive effects:

    a.   Test interpretive hypotheses (disambiguation, reference res-
         olution, implicatures, etc.) in order of accessibility.
    b.   Stop when your expectations of relevance are satisfied (or
         abandoned).

This is not to be understood as something like a Gricean maxim which
we are expected to follow when understanding something. Rather, it
is a generalisation about what we actually do. It follows from underlyingly rational principles, like Grice's approach, but it is a claim about
what we do and the theory no longer assumes a step-by-step reasoning
process like the one suggested by Grice.

What we do, then, is to look in order of accessibility for possible
interpretations and assume that interpretations which lead to effects
which justify that effort are ones intended by the communicator
(provided they could and would have intended such an interpretation).
We can illustrate this with reference to this example:

    (8) Adam: Has Dani paid you back yet?
         Bella: She didn't make it to the bank today.

Here Adam will look for a referent for *she* and of course Dani is a
very salient possibility. He then needs to decide which sense of *bank*
is intended. The 'financial institution' sense should be quite accessible
and of course this will lead to positive cognitive effects since Adam
can now infer that (Bella is saying that) Dani must not have paid Bella
back as she didn't manage to get money. This also implicates that Dani
would have paid Bella back if she had been able to go the bank.

There are of course other possible interpretations for this utterance
and others would be more likely if Adam accessed different contextual
assumptions. Suppose, for example, that Adam knows that Bella is
exasperated with Dani because she never pays back debts, is generally
unreliable, and often makes excuses. In this situation, Adam might
access assumptions about Dani's general unreliableness and decide that
Bella is not happy about what's happened and sees Dani as producing
another excuse and being disappointing again. Adam will reach this
interpretation if these assumptions are accessible and both Adam and
Bella are aware that they share them.

Overall, then, the relevance-theoretic account is based on ideas about a technical notion of relevance and the fairly specific expectations about relevance which arise when we recognise an act of ostensive communication. The relevance-guided comprehension heuristic is a process which follows from these and which we automatically follow whenever we recognise an ostensive act.

EXPLICATURES AND IMPLICATURES

Relevance theory also proposes a different way of thinking about what can be directly or indirectly communicated.

EXPLICATURE

Grice drew a distinction between saying and implicating but he did not say much about saying and only mentioned two processes, disambiguation and reference assignment, involved in recovering what is said. He also made no comment on what was involved in disambiguation and reference assignment. Later pragmaticists recognised that these must also be pragmatic processes, based on contextual assumptions and constrained by pragmatic principles. Early work on relevance theory (e.g. Wilson and Sperber 1981) focused on this, suggesting that pragmatic processes must be involved in working out 'what is said' by an utterance. Here are two examples which illustrate this:

(9) Adam: Can we hold the meeting even though Calum isn't here.

Bella: Dani can be the chair.

(10) Adam: I thought we might ask Calum to chair the meeting?

Bella: He's not well today.

In (9), we are likely to take the meaning of *chair* to be the one that refers to somebody who is in charge of a meeting. While the kinds of chairs we sit on are associated with meetings, it is hard to see how Bella's utterance would lead to enough effects if we took that to be the intended meaning here. In relevance-theoretic terms, assuming the sense of being in charge of the meeting leads to enough effects to justify the effort of interpreting the utterance and this would not be possible on the other interpretation (the bizarre one in which Bella is suggesting that Dani can be something to sit on).

In (10), we are likely to think of Calum as the referent of *he*. In Grice's terms, if Bella meant somebody else, she would either not be informative enough or not relevant if she did not say so. In relevance-theoretic terms, assuming that the referent is Calum leads to enough effects to justify the effort involved in interpreting the utterance, and there is nothing to suggest that Bella could not or would not have meant this.

Relevance theory goes further than this. It seems that working out what is 'said' or directly communicated by an utterance often involves more than just disambiguation and reference assignment. In fact, it's not clear that we could list all of the kinds of things we might need to infer to arrive at this. Consider these examples:

(11) I can if you want me to.
(12) In these shoes?

The speaker here has chosen not to include linguistic material which could have been uttered and we need to make inferences about what it was in order to work out what proposition the utterances represent and directly communicate. The term for this is 'ellipsis' and these are usually called 'elliptical' utterances.

In (11), as well as working out the referents of *I* and *you* and the sense of *can* (here a modal verb indicating ability and/or willingness), we need to work out who is the person who can do something (the speaker is the most likely, of course) and what it is that they can do if the addressee wants them to. (We'll leave aside vagueness about what *want* means here.)

In (12) (the title of a song by Kirsty McColl), we need to infer not just the referent of *these shoes* and what exactly *in* means. We also need to infer most of the proposition. Leaving aside some details (trusting you to make inferences and follow what I mean), it could, for example be something like (13), (14), or (15):

(13) Do you think I can go to my job interview wearing these shoes?
(14) Are you suggesting that I can walk up that muddy hill wearing these shoes?
(15) Is the orthopaedic insole you mentioned inside these shoes?

There are also cases where we seem to make inferences that go beyond 'filling in gaps' (as in ellipsis) indicated by linguistic forms.

An early discussion of this (Wilson and Sperber 1981) focused on this example, uttered when the speaker and hearer are watching John playing a violin:

(16) John plays well.

To understand what's directly communicated here, we need to decide who *John* refers to and work out which sense of the ambiguous expression *play* (e.g. play a game, play a musical instrument) is intended. If we do both of these we will work out that the John referred to plays a musical instrument well, i.e. (17):

(17) John plays some musical instrument well.

However, it is clear that this is not what the speaker intends here. The hearer will infer not only that John plays some musical instrument or instruments well but (18):

(18) John plays the violin well.

Other kinds of cases include:

(19) Adam: How was the party?
     Bella: There wasn't enough drink and everyone left early.

As Carston and Hall (2012) point out, Adam will infer here that:

(20) The party did not go well.

This is clearly an implicature as it is inferred on the basis of the conjunction of the two propositions directly communicated. Carston and Hall suggest that what is directly communicated is not simply the conjunction in (21):

(21) The party did not go well. Everyone left early.

Instead, the hearer will infer extra material and arrive at a conjoined proposition like (22):

(22) There wasn't enough **alcoholic drink** at the party **to satisfy everyone who came to the party** and everyone **who came to the party** left the party early.

(Ignoring for now that Adam needs to infer which party is being referred to), the parts in bold here need to be inferred in order to understand what Bella is communicating but there is no linguistic indication that we need to infer them.

Another example which has often been discussed (including by Kent Bach 1994) is an utterance like (23) said to a child who is crying after cutting their finger:

(23) You're not going to die.

The child here needs to work out that the speaker means that they are not going to die as a result of the cut. It is hard to see how we could argue that this follows from the linguistic meaning of *die* or of anything else in the linguistic expression.

On this approach, some things which Grice would have treated as implicatures are treated as part of what is directly communicated. For relevance theory, this means that they are part of what they term an **explicature**. The view is not that these propositions are wholly explicitly communicated. Rather, they are partly explicit (since parts of them are part of the linguistic meaning) and partly implicit (since parts of them need to be inferred). The '*-cature*' part of the ending, of course, is the same as the ending of *implicature* so we can understand this as establishing a convention where words ending with *-cature* represent things that are intentionally communicated.

One thing which follows from this account is that communicated assumptions which Grice's account would have seen as implicatures are now seen as parts of explicatures. Rather than inferring two propositions as in (24) and (25), the claim is that the causal connection in (25) is part of the explicature of the utterance as represented in (26):

(24) There was not enough drink. Everyone left early.
(25) Everyone left early because there was not enough drink.
(26) There wasn't enough **alcoholic drink** at the party **to satisfy everyone who came to the party** and **as a result of the lack of alcoholic drink** everyone **who came to the party** left the party early.

EXPLICATURES WITHIN EXPLICATURES

Explicatures can also contain propositions embedded under other propositions. Consider the exchange in (27):

(27) Adam: Did Dani say anything about me when you saw her?
Bella: That haircut really suits you.

Adam could understand Bella to be saying that Dani said that Adam's haircut really suits him or he could infer that she is expressing her own thought (rather than answering his question). These two interpretations differ with regard to who is seen as thinking or saying that Adam's haircut suits him. We can represent these possibilities as (28) and (29):

(28) Bella is saying that
Dani said that
Adam's haircut really suits Adam
(29) Bella is saying that
Adam's haircut really suits Adam

(28) involves one more layer than (29) since Bella is saying that Dani said something rather than just saying something herself. We can imagine further embeddings, e.g. in response to a question like (30) which could lead to the assumption in (31):

(30) What did Eddie say that Dani said?
(31) Bella said that
Eddie said that
Dani said that
Adam's haircut really suits Adam

And so on. Relevance theory calls explicatures like these, which embed other propositions within them, **higher-level explicatures**.

The notion of higher-level explicatures plays a role in the relevance-theoretic account of irony where ironic utterances are seen as presenting some of the lower-level propositions as ones which speakers attribute to others and dissociate themselves from.

Suppose, for example, that Adam says this to Bella:

(32) I've arranged for a new plumber to fix the shower tomorrow. He's really reliable.

If the plumber turns out to be reliable, Bella might paraphrase what Adam said with a positive attitude to this idea:

(33) Wow! He IS reliable!

As well as communicating that she thinks the new plumber is reliable, Bella can be seen as communicating a positive higher-level explicature such as (34):

(34) Bella thinks that
    Adam was right to think that
        the plumber Adam hired is reliable

If the plumber never shows up, or disappears without completing the job, Bella might still say (33) but this time she will be understood not only as attributing the thought that the plumber is reliable to Adam but also (implicitly) dissociating herself from the idea. The idea developed within relevance theory is that utterances are ironic when the speaker is understood as attributing the thought their utterance represents to others and dissociating themself from it.

The 'others' to whom the thought is attributed might not be very clearly identifiable. In some cases, they can be representing thoughts which people might generally want to express rather than echoing any specific person's thought or utterance, such as classic ironical utterances about the weather or public transport as in (35) and (36):

(35) *(on a rainy day)* What lovely weather!
(36) *(at a bus stop when buses are seriously delayed)* Our public transport system is so wonderful!

NO CONVENTIONAL IMPLICATURES

Relevance theory, like other pragmatic theories, does not adopt the notion of conventional implicatures. Many pragmaticists have noticed problems with this notion. 'Conventional' is understood here as referring to linguistic meanings and it is surprising to hear that some implicatures are part of linguistic meaning. This seems contradictory and, if we adopt it, we need to do more than simply state that some expressions generate implicatures. This raises questions about what kind of linguistic meaning is involved and how these meanings arise.

In an influential discussion, Kent Bach (1999) suggested that the notion of conventional implicature 'throws a monkey wrench' into Grice's semantics-pragmatics distinction and that this monkey wrench 'needs to be removed'. Within relevance theory, Diane Blakemore (1987, 2002) developed the idea that some expressions have meanings which constrain inferential processes. This led to the development of the notion of 'procedural meaning'. This is a complex notion. Simplifying considerably, the idea is that some expressions affect how we process utterances rather than identifying concepts.

Nouns like *vegan*, *carnivore*, *meat*, and *food* have conceptual meanings. When we hear an utterance with these words, we access related concepts and (usually) add them to explicatures. We can say the same for verbs like *eat*, *love*, and *avoid*, and for adjectives like *vegan* (this word is ambiguous between a noun and adjective sense, of course), *carnivorous*, *raw*, and *spicy*. We can explain the difference between (37) and (38) by referring to different conceptual meanings for *vegan* and *carnivorous*:

(37) Calum is vegan.
(38) Calum is carnivorous.

Blakemore suggested that some words do not affect the conceptual representations derived from utterances but the inferences we draw from them. Consider (39) and (40):

(39) Calum is vegan and he loves spicy food.
(40) Calum is vegan but he loves spicy food.

(39) says that Calum is vegan and that he loves spicy food. (40) also communicates both of these assumptions. The word *but*, though, has a significant impact on the interpretation. Blakemore would suggest that it leads the hearer to look for some conclusions they could infer from the first conjunct (that Calum is vegan) and to eliminate them. This leads to the understanding that the speaker must think, for some reason, that people who are vegan don't usually like spicy food. This is not present in (39) where the utterance includes the conjunction *and* rather than *but*.

Interestingly, (39) could be seen to be contradicting the idea that vegan people don't usually like spicy food (an interpretation which could be made more likely by particular ways of saying it) but this assumption does not follow directly from any of the linguistic expressions.

The idea that some expressions have procedural meanings offers a new way of accounting for many of the cases which Grice viewed as conventional implicatures.

NO GENERALISED CONVERSATIONAL IMPLICATURES

Relevance theory does not assume a distinction between generalised and particularised conversational implicatures. It sees all implicatures as arising from the search for an interpretation guided by the assumed comprehension heuristic. In all cases, hearers follow a path of least effort in looking for interpretations which meet their expectations of relevance. In some cases, these correspond to what Grice saw as generalised conversational implicatures. The theory assumes that there is no need to distinguish implicatures which 'generally' arise 'by default' from those which arise because of specific contextual assumptions. All implicatures are seen as arising in the same way.

Some things which would count as generalised conversational implicatures for Grice are treated as parts of explicatures, such as the following, where the part which would be seen as a generalised conversational implicature is in [square brackets]:

(41) He turned the key and [as a result of him turning the key] the engine started.

ONLY ONE TYPE OF IMPLICATURE

On this approach (developed by Robyn Carston) the causal connection between the two propositions is seen as part of the explicature of this utterance rather than as a separate implicature.

It's less clear how to deal with some of the other cases which Grice treated as generalised conversational implicatures such as (42) and (43):

(42) Some of the students enjoyed the class.
      Possible implicature:
      Not all of the students enjoyed the class.

(43) I saw a beautiful house yesterday.
      Possible implicature:
      The house was not the speaker's house.

In each case, it would be possible to embed the extra information into explicatures such as (44) or (45):

(44) Some [but not all] of the students enjoyed the class.
(45) I saw a beautiful house [which was not my own].

However, it's not clear whether this is what individuals do when understanding utterances like this. They might instead, as suggested by Grice, derive these as separate implicatures. Within a relevance-theoretic approach, then, these could be treated either as parts of explicatures or as separate implicatures.

Since these inferences are not seen as automatically made by 'default', they might not always be made. When they are assumed, it is because they arise as part of the process of working out intended meanings following the comprehension heuristic. Someone who is wondering whether all of the students enjoyed the class is likely to assume that they didn't all enjoy it when they hear that 'some' did. Where this is not relevant (or ruled out by some contextual assumptions), and where the utterance is relevant without making this assumption, then they won't make it. This might help to account for variation among different addressees. If I gave the class referred to, I am likely to be hoping that all of the students enjoyed the class and so I am likely to flesh out the explicature in this way. Somebody who is less concerned about the class and the response of the students might not think of this.

STRONGER AND WEAKER IMPLICATURES

Another feature of relevance theory is the idea that communicated assumptions can be more or less strongly communicated. Assumptions are not seen simply as either communicated or not. Rather, an utterance or communicative act provides more or less evidence for particular conclusions. Let's return to Bella's utterance '*he's vegan*'. So far, we have focused on implicatures which this utterance supports very strongly, in particular the assumption that Calum will not want any of the cake which Adam is referring to. Notice, however, that Bella's utterance provides evidence for a range of conclusions, arguably including the following:

(46) Calum will not want any of the cake Adam is asking about.
(47) Calum will not want to eat anything with meat in it.
(48) Calum will not want to eat anything containing dairy products.
(49) Calum will not want to use toiletries whose production has affected animals.
(50) Calum cares about the planet.
(51) Calum has a strong moral compass.

You probably think that some of these are more likely to have been communicated than others. They are roughly ordered with regard to this. (46) is the most strongly communicated. In fact, it is hard to see how we could claim that Adam has understood Bella's utterance if he does not infer this. Bella's utterance gives at least some evidence for the others. Even someone who know very little about veganism would be likely to know that vegans avoid eating meat and dairy products and so understand that (47) and (48) follow from Calum being vegan. Not everyone will know that vegans generally avoid toiletries whose production involves animals. If Adam assumes this (and thinks that Bella both assumes it and assumes that Adam assumes it), then he will infer (49). (50) and (51) are weaker in that it is possible to be vegan and not to care about the planet and also not to have a strong moral compass. Still, if Adam thinks about this, he is likely to assume that Bella provided some evidence for them.

The fact that we can be more or less sure about whether particular implicatures are intended is a key idea in relevance theory and plays a role in accounts of range of kinds of interpretations, including metaphorical interpretations and impressionistic communication.

Explicatures too can be more or less strongly communicated but this has not been focused on as often. We could, for example, consider utterances which mainly contain just one noun phrase, such as these:

(52) Oh, life!
(53) Kids, eh?
(54) Football! Bloody hell!

The speaker of (52) is giving evidence for a wide range of assumptions about life, e.g. that it is difficult, that it is complicated, and so on. Similarly, (53) suggests a range of things that the speaker could be thinking about kids and/or about being a parent or carer of kids. (54) was uttered after a football match in 1999 by the Manchester United manager, Alex Ferguson. Again, there are a range of things he is suggesting about football: that it is amazing, surprising, unpredictable, emotional, and so on. The speaker in each case gives some evidence for a wide range of possible explicatures but we can't be sure exactly which ones they have in mind.

LIMITING INTERPRETATIONS

An important part of relevance theory is how it rules out certain possible interpretations. Sperber and Wilson (1986) demonstrate this by considering how we might interpret the word *cat* in an everyday context. While it might not occur to you right away, the word *cat* has more than one sense in English, including two which refer to feline animals. It can refer to the kind of domesticated cat which I am likely to see as I go about my day in Newcastle and it also has a broader sense which covers all members of the cat family.

Imagine I say this to a friend while we are sitting in my office at work:

(55) There's a big cat outside.

The first (domesticated cat) sense is likely to occur to my friend quite quickly and lead to enough effects to justify processing my utterance. It indicates that there is an everyday kind of cat outside, that my friend might want to look outside if she's interested in cats, and not much else. Suppose that I meant the broader sense of *cat*. What if there was something outside like a tiger or a leopard? That would be much more relevant. It would contradict some of my friend's existing assumptions (about the likelihood of seeing animals like that in Newcastle) and suggest some significant new assumptions (including that people outside are in danger). However, my friend will not go for an interpretation like this and this follows from the Communicative Principle of Relevance and the comprehension heuristic. The 'domesticated cat' sense will be accessed first as I follow a path of least effort and meet my friend's expectations of relevance. My friend will not look for any further possible interpretations.

The relevance-theoretic account also explains why small changes in the amount of effort involved in processing an utterance can have quite significant effects. Consider these two possible utterances:

(56) a. How are you?
     b. How are you these days?

Most people think that (56b) suggests more interest from the speaker in exactly how the hearer is doing than (56a). The relevance-the-oretic account says that the extra effort involved in processing *these days* leads to these effects. In most circumstances, the hearer of (56a) will assume that the question is about how the hearer is doing around the time of utterance. So *these days* does not affect that. The extra effort has to lead to some effects, though, and something like greater interest in the hearer's wellbeing is a natural assumption. This kind of account applies to a range of examples like this, where a slight increase in the effort required to process an utterance leads to a significant change in the interpretation. Repetitions are interesting examples. Here are some examples discussed by Sperber and Wilson (1995: 219):

(57) a. *(while sorting laundry)* Here's a blue sock, here's a blue sock, here's a red sock, …
     b. There were houses, houses everywhere.
     c. There's a fox, a fox in the garden.
     d. My childhood days are gone, gone.

The repetitions here have different kinds of effects. The extra effort involved in processing the repeated word leads the hearer to look for further effects (more than they would have found without the rep-etition). They look in order or accessibility and stop when they find enough effects to justify the effort. In (57a), they will assume simply that the speaker has picked up another blue sock. In (57b), the speaker is communicating that there were lots of houses and a little bit more about the experience of seeing them, as we can see by considering how we would interpret (58) or (59):

(58) There were lots of houses.
(59) There were lots of houses everywhere.

(57c) suggests that the speaker is surprised about the fox. (57d) encourages the hearer to think about the emotional state of the speaker, perhaps imagining what they feel like as they think back to their childhood days. With no more straightforward interpretation along the lines possible for (57a–c), the hearer is likely to be creative in imagining the speaker's emotional state. The hearer is likely to access a relatively wide range of relatively weak implicatures here. Relevance theorists have suggested that this is typical of what have been called 'poetic effects' where the precise interpretation of an utterance is hard to pin down. 'Poetic effects' are not only associated with poetry but with any kind of utterance which gives rise to a wide range of possible interpretations.

FINDING OUT MORE

Here are some ideas for things you might do to develop understanding of ideas in the chapter and to find out more, followed by some suggested further reading.

YOUR OWN EXAMPLES

For this chapter, examples you focus on could include making a note of things you think addressees are likely to assume from particular communicative acts and categorising them. Within relevance theory, this will mean deciding whether they are explicatures, implicatures, or non-communicated implications. The next step, of course, is to see whether you can explain them with reference to the relevance-guided comprehension heuristic, which means showing how they follow from a search for effects following a path of least effort.

COMPARING APPROACHES

Another useful exercise you could try is to compare how different approaches would account for particular examples. You might, for example, look at examples you have discussed before and consider how different approaches would account for them. You could do this with the examples you looked at after reading previous chapters or new ones you have identified now. You might also look at examples I have discussed in this chapter.

SOME MORE SPECIFIC QUESTIONS

As ever, it's important to think critically when developing and evaluating pragmatic theories. In considering the relevance-theoretic approach discussed here, you might consider whether there are gaps in the explanation. Two critical comments which have been made about relevance theory (both of which have also been made about Grice's approach and neo-Gricean theories) are:

a. That it focuses mainly on what addressees do and does not say much about the role of communicators or how all of the people in an interaction work together to create meanings and interpretations

b. That it mainly focuses on individual utterances or pairs of utterances rather than looking at how interpretations develop during an extended exchange

You could consider each of these questions and, if you agree with the criticism, consider how relevance theory could be changed to address it.

POEMS AND SONGS

Poems and songs are always interesting examples to analyse. Choose a poem or song whose words you like and consider how relevance theory might account for aspects of their interpretation. You might consider different ways of thinking about pronouns, as discussed in this chapter, consider how words are used with more than one meaning, or consider how the understanding of a particular word changes during a song. Finally, of course, it is always interesting to identify particular implicatures and consider how listeners arrive at them.

FURTHER READING

The most accessible texts by Sperber and Wilson on relevance theory are:

1. Sperber, Dan and Deirdre Wilson. 2005b. Pragmatics. In F. Jackson and M. Smith (eds.) *Oxford Handbook of Philosophy of Language*, Oxford University Press: 468–501.
2. Wilson, Deirdre. 2017. Relevance theory. In Y. Huang (ed.) *The Oxford Handbook of Pragmatics*. Oxford University Press: 79–100.

3.   Wilson, Deirdre. 2019. Relevance theory. In *Oxford Research Encyclopedia of Linguistics*. Oxford University Press. http://dx.doi.org /10.1093/acrefore/9780199384655.013.201

4.   Wilson, Deirdre and Dan Sperber. 2004. Relevance theory. In L. Horn and G. Ward (eds.) *The Handbook of Pragmatics*. Wiley-Blackwell: 607–632.

A brief introductory textbook is:

5.   Blakemore, Diane. 2002. *Understanding Utterances: An Introduction to Pragmatics*. Wiley-Blackwell.

A more comprehensive textbook is:

6.   Clark, Billy. 2013. *Relevance Theory*. Cambridge University Press.

A comprehensive discussion of key ideas from relevance theory is:

7.   Carston, Robyn. 2002. *Thoughts and Utterances*. Wiley-Blackwell.

A comprehensive and regularly updated bibliography of work on relevance theory, maintained and updated by Francisco Yus:

8.   Relevance Theory Online Bibliographic Service. https://personal.ua. es/francisco.yus/rt.html

MANAGING INTERACTION (IM)POLITENESS

This chapter considers another key area of pragmatics, which focuses on how we manage social relationships in interaction and, more specifically, on how utterances can be more or less polite. Being more or less polite is only part of what's involved in managing social relationships but it's an area which has been focused on very much over the years, and research on politeness has led to broader questions about what we might focus on when considering social interaction in general.

Early work in this area treated politeness as something which sometimes affects what we say or do in communicating. More recent work has acknowledged both that all communicative behaviour is more or less polite and that we sometimes formulate things with the intention of being **im**polite. Work in this area is now sometimes referred to as being about developing '(im)politeness' (or 'im/politeness') theories.

BEING (IM)POLITE IN VERBAL INTERACTIONS

It is easy to find examples of communicative behaviour which we understand as more or less polite. We often talk explicitly about what kinds of behaviour are considered polite or not and we are aware of cultural differences with regard to this. We can also see this in everyday exchanges. Which of the following responses do you think I would be most likely to give if a colleague at work asked if I would like a coffee?

    (1) No.

    (2) No thanks.

    (3) Oh, no thanks. I've just had one actually. Thanks for offering.

I am guessing that you think (3) is the most polite option. Why is this? (1) simply communicates that I don't want coffee. (2) communicates this and also thanks my colleague for the offer. (3) also gives a reason for me not accepting the offer.

A natural way to discuss the differences is to consider the possible implicatures of each response (arguably, some of these are implications if we decide that the speaker is not taken to be communicating them intentionally). (1) risks giving rise to implicatures such as that my colleague doesn't understand me very well and that my only interest here is in rejecting the offer. (2) thanks the colleague in a conventional way but the fact that this is so conventional means that it doesn't do much more than (1) to indicate any concern for my colleague's feelings. By giving a reason for me not wanting coffee, (3) both reduces the risk of negative implicatures and indicates that I do care about my colleague's feelings. This seems a reasonable way to begin to account for the varying politeness of these utterances.

These examples can also be used to illustrate some of the ways in which what counts as polite is different in different contexts. (2) might not be seen as rude if I know my colleague very well, i.e. if we are close enough for questions about our relationship not to be salient. (1) or (2) are responses which might seem completely typical if the conversation is between a couple who live together. We can also illustrate cultural variation with examples. In some cultural contexts, any of these responses would be likely to lead to a repeated offer while in others the negative response would be accepted.

There are lots of different kinds of examples which suggest that we should say something about politeness when explaining interaction.

    (4) Adam: I'm not sure I'm up to delivering my class today.
           Bella: Would you like me to cover it for you?
           Adam: That would be fantastic. Thank you!

Adam could have asked Bella directly whether she might be able to cover his class for him but instead mentions that it will be difficult for him. The result is that Bella offers to cover the class for him but without him having asked directly and so clearly imposing on her. This could be understood as an indirect request; the fact that the request is not explicit means that Adam can (arguably) deny that he intended the request.

In other cases, speakers are indirect in refusing offers or requests. Consider (3), for example:

> (5) Adam: Do you want to go and see *Parasite* tomorrow evening?
>
> Bella: I'd love to but I'm afraid I've got something else on.

Bella might not have other plans but it is safer to provide a reason for not being able to go to the cinema rather than simply saying no, which would seem quite impolite (as we saw in the first example above).

Notice that a straightforward negative response seems to follow the maxims more closely than the longer answers. They are brief, informative, and don't give too much information. It seems, then, that there are separate motivations for saying more and generating implicatures.

EARLY APPROACHES: LAKOFF, LEECH, BROWN AND LEVINSON

I mentioned Leech's approach to politeness in Chapter 3 as an example of an approach which suggested adding more maxims to the ones proposed by Grice. Another early approach which suggested increasing the number of new maxims assumed was developed by Robin Lakoff. Lakoff, like Leech, suggested a new Politeness Principle. This one had three maxims: don't impose; give the receiver options; make the receiver feel good. As we saw, Leech suggested a greater number of new maxims. Leech and Lakoff shared the view that there were things which affected what we say other than those reflected in Grice's Cooperative Principle and maxims.

Also in the 1970s, Penelope Brown and Stephen Levinson made a very influential contribution by relating ideas about politeness to the notion of 'face', which they took from the sociologist and social psychologist Erving Goffman. Goffman produced a huge amount of work on human behaviour, interaction, and other topics. He also suggested that we could understand a range of aspects of human interaction with reference to the notion of 'face', which originates in Chinese cultures and relates to an individual's standing within a cultural group. In many cultures, this notion is referred to in informal discussion of behaviour. English speakers, for example, talk about doing things to 'save face' or to avoid 'losing face'. Roughly, the notion of face has to do with how we are viewed within a culture as more or less respectable, with more or less of a good reputation or esteem, and so on. Sometimes this is referred to as social 'value'. Goffman discussed various kinds of 'facework' we engage in to protect or enhance our own and other people's social value.

Brown and Levinson adopted this notion in developing an account of how we can be more or less polite in interactions. Brown and Levinson's work was extremely influential and the main motivation for what has since been described as the 'first wave' of work on politeness.

To understand Brown and Levinson's approach, we need to consider a number of key components of their approach as well as the notion of face itself: a distinction between positive and negative face, the recognition of 'face-threatening acts', and a number of strategies which we adopt in interactions and which have an impact on face.

POSITIVE AND NEGATIVE FACE

Brown and Levinson's approach assumes a distinction between positive face and negative face. While their definitions changed over time, the general idea is that some of our face 'needs' or 'wants' are about wanting to seem important and valued (positive face wants) while others are about wanting **not** to be impeded, constrained, etc. (negative face wants). One (earlier) way of defining them is as follows:

positive face: the want of every member that his wants be desirable to at least some others

negative face: the want of every 'competent adult member' that his actions be unimpeded by others

(Brown and Levinson 1987: 62)

We are addressing somebody's positive face needs when we compliment them or offer them something. We are addressing their negative needs when we avoid imposing on them or limiting their options.

A nonverbal example which arguably addresses both simultaneously would be moving aside to let somebody past on a tube train. By letting them through, we are showing that we see them as important, that their wants are desired, and that we are avoiding impeding them.

Brown and Levinson's approach focuses on verbal examples and assumes that polite behaviour occurs when a communicator becomes aware that they are at risk of doing something which might go against the face wants of others.

FACE-THREATENING ACTS

While we often aim to address the positive and negative face wants of others, sometimes we do or say things which risk threatening one or the other of these. Behaviours which do this are termed 'face-threatening acts' (often abbreviated to 'FTAs') by Brown and Levinson. They can lead to adjustments in how we phrase utterances. These are designed to reduce the risk of 'face damage'. Of course, these can be categorised according to whether they threaten the other person's positive or negative face.

Acts which threaten positive face are ones which go against the desire of an individual to have their wants be desirable to others, including wanting to be admired, respected, and so on. Threats to positive face will include negative comments on aspects of that person (e.g. their clothes, looks, behaviour, desires). One example would involve directly or indirectly criticising somebody's clothes or appearance:

(6) Those shoes are horrible.
(7) You're not really going out looking like that, are you?

To reduce the risk of threatening the other person's face, a speaker might say something they don't really believe, e.g. saying that the shoes look good, or they might choose instead to say something more tentative such as:

(8) They're lovely. I'm just wondering how well they go with that outfit.

(9) You look great. I don't have the confidence to carry that look off, though.

In some contexts, an utterance might threaten the speaker's own positive face, e.g. by admitting a mistake or apologising. This shows, of course, that sometimes addressing the face wants of the speaker will be in conflict with addressing the face wants of the hearer. For example, avoiding an apology, to minimise threat to the speaker's own face, can threaten the hearer's face by suggesting that the hearer's wants are not important and/or or not being addressed (or maybe suggesting that the hearer has made a mistake). If I aim to prioritise my addressee's wants, then I am likely to apologise. If I care more about my own face, then I might not. Of course, there are options which are a compromise between the two. I might, for example, apologise but also say something to explain why I made the mistake.

Acts which threaten negative face are ones which threaten an individual's desire to have their actions unimpeded by others. Threats to negative face will include requests, impositions, and other acts which constrain or attempt to constrain the hearer's behaviour. Offers and promises can also count as they offer to help the speaker now but imply a future imposition.

Again, there can be tensions here between the communicator's and the addressee's wants. Asking you to help me threatens your negative face wants but not doing so threatens mine (since I will have to change my behaviour to address the issue).

POLITENESS STRATEGIES

A key feature of Brown and Levinson's approach is their focus on strategies which we use to address the face wants of other people. This is an example of what Goffman called 'facework'.

One option a speaker has when they realise that they might be about to commit a face-threatening act is not to perform the act at all. If you meet me and I look really tired and not very well, you might choose not to say anything rather than commenting. Commenting on my appearance would highlight negative aspects of this and also suggest that my want to be thought of in a positive light is not very important to you.

If you decide to perform the act anyway, perhaps because you think the threat is not too great (maybe we are very close and feel safe to share details of our lives, including negative aspects, with each other), you can then choose either to perform the act 'on record' (i.e. explicitly) or 'off record' (implicitly).

If you decide to go on record, you might say something as strong as (10) or the slightly weaker (11):

(10) You look terrible!
(11) You're not looking your best today, are you?

If you decide to go off record, you might just ask me a general question such as (12):

(12) How's everything with you?

With on record acts, there is also a distinction between 'bald' acts and acts which include some 'redressive action' to reduce the face threat.

(13) I'm sorry to say this but you're not looking your best today, are you?

These categories apply to threats to the speaker as well as to the hearer. If a colleague asks me whether I can do something to help them, there is some threat to my face if I agree too quickly to do it, suggesting that I am putting their needs above my own, as in (14):

(14) Sure!

So I might go off record and say something like (15):

(15) I think I might have time to do that later today. Can I just check and get back to you?

We can understand these options as being in a hierarchy. The most risky option is to perform a face-threatening act baldly and on record. The next most risky option is to perform the act on record but including features which redress the act to some extent. If this seems too risky, then we can perform the act off record. Finally, if we do not think it is worth the risk at all, we can say nothing. Here are a range of options arranged in this order for how an individual might react if their friend arrives to meet them with a nasty bruise on their face:

(16) **(bald on record)**
Wow, that's a nasty bruise!
(17) **(on record with redress)**
I'm sorry, but can I just say, that looks pretty nasty.
(18) **(off record)**
Hi, how are things with you?
(19) **(not performed)**
(no mention or only indirect reference)

Brown and Levinson also discuss some factors which affect the 'weight' or seriousness of a face-threatening act. They focus on the social 'distance' between interlocutors, the power relationships between them, and the relative ranking within a culture of the kinds of impositions we might make on each other. In fact, Brown and Levinson even propose this formula to account for the 'weight' of a particular face-threatening act (where W stands for 'weightiness', D for social distance, P for power, and R for ranking):

$$Wx = D\ (S,H) + P\ (S,H) + Rx$$

Brown and Levinson's work has been extremely influential and was the dominant approach to politeness until at least the mid-1990s. There are now significantly more approaches to accounting for politeness phenomena. The next two sections consider more recent developments.

(IM)POLITENESS EVERYWHERE

One significant development in work on politeness is the recognition that every time we interact with others we are more or less polite to them. As I walk down the street, I can give more or less distance to other people passing me by. If I give them a lot of space, then I am addressing their positive and negative face wants (positive by treating their wants as important, negative by not impeding them). Of course, giving them too much space, e.g. stepping into the road when only one person is approaching on the pavement, would threaten my own face, by undervaluing my own wants, and perhaps threaten the other person's face if understood as a sarcastic exaggeration. The more I block them, the more impolite I am, and so on.

Similarly, every verbal interaction can be assessed for how polite it is, rather than seeing politeness phenomena as things which sometimes affect how an utterance is formulated. Consider the very first example in Chapter 1 of this book:

> (20) *A man (Adam) walks into a room where a television is switched on. He picks up the remote and turns the television off. He then turns around and sees a woman (Bella) sitting in an armchair.*
> Bella: I was watching that!

I didn't mention politeness at all when discussing this earlier but of course Bella's utterance can be seen as potentially face-threatening. By simply saying that she was watching the TV, she is suggesting that her own wants should be important enough for Adam not to have switched it off (and for him to apologise and turn it on again). This counts as an off record strategy since she has simply stated that she was watching the TV and Adam has to infer that he should not have done this and that Bella expects him to do something about his mistake.

An on record response could have been:

> (21)   Turn that back on.

Equally, Bella could have been more polite, saying, for example:

> (22)   I'm sorry, Adam. I was watching that. Would you mind turning it back on?

This would be an on record strategy with some redress of the face-threatening aspects.

Bella could also, of course, have decided not to perform the act at all and just accepted that she would not be watching the TV from now on.

We can assess the politeness of every interaction, even something which seems very straightforward, such as this example which we have returned to several times:

(23) Adam: Do you think Calum would like a piece of this cake?
      Bella: He's vegan.

Bella could have been more polite by adding some features which reduce the risk of this seeming to function as a reprimand to Adam for not realising that Calum wouldn't want any cake and/or implying he has made a mistake. She might, for example, have said:

(24) Oh, I must have forgotten to tell you. Calum's vegan so he won't want any.

Or she could have been much less polite and said something like:

(25) Don't be stupid. Of course he won't. He's vegan!

When we recognise that aspects of politeness are relevant to all interactions, it is not surprising that work on politeness (and impoliteness) has increased over the years and that a very large amount of work in pragmatics has focused on this.

(IM)POLITENESS

Early work on politeness focused on strategies we can adopt in situations which raise the possibility of a face-threatening act being performed, and it considered how actions or behaviours could be more or less polite, with some being seen as definitely impolite. During the 1990s, attention began to focus on behaviour which was intended to be impolite. It is clear that some 'facework' is designed to attack the face of others rather than to address their face wants. In some work, acts which do this are described as 'face-aggravating' acts.

A number of ideas have been focused on in exploring impoliteness. As always in pragmatics, key questions are about whether an act is intentionally impolite and whether that intention is communicated. There are socially important differences between acts which are accidentally impolite, acts which are intentionally but not overtly impolite, and acts which are clearly and intentionally impolite:

(26) How's the essay going?
(27) You're really useless. You're taking ages over that essay!

(26) could threaten my face without the speaker intending this. If, for example, the speaker has no intentions or assumptions about how my essay is going and the essay is going badly, then I am put into the difficult position of having to admit that things are not going well or find another way to respond (I might lie, for example, or change the subject). Of course, the speaker might suspect or even know that the essay is going badly but assume that I don't know they know this. In this case, the face-threatening act is performed intentionally but the intention to damage my face is not overtly communicated. (27), of course, is a direct and blatant face-aggravating act.

Culpeper (1996: 356–357) identifies a number of impoliteness strategies. In '**bald on record**' impoliteness, a face-threatening act is clearly and directly performed in a context where questions about face are 'not irrelevant or minimised' (to rule out cases where questions of politeness don't arise, e.g. when 'communicating' with a computer). (27) is a clear example.

Positive impoliteness strategies are ones which aim to damage somebody else's positive face wants. There are, of course, lots of ways to do this, including ignoring somebody, pretending not to know them (or remember their name), leaving uncomfortable silences, and so on.

Negative impoliteness strategies aim to damage another person's negative face wants. Again, there are lots of ways to do this, including physical ones such as space invasion (Culpeper points out that this can be metaphorical too, e.g. asking for information that is too intimate), saying things which suggest something will happen which the other person doesn't want, emphasising power relations (where you have more power), reminding somebody they owe you something, and so on.

'**Off record impoliteness**' is, of course, implicated impoliteness. We can consider, here, how strongly particular impolite implicatures are communicated. We could differentiate, for example, cases where I am very clearly impolite from ones where an impolite implicature occurs but it is not so strongly communicated. Compare, for example, two ways I could respond if you ask to borrow money from me:

(28) OK, I can manage that if it's just for a few days.
(29) Sure. Here you go.

The first very clearly implicates an obligation on you to repay me. The second simply agrees, but of course the debt is now established.

There are also '**withhold politeness**' strategies, where somebody does not do 'politeness work' where it would be expected. Imagine, for example, if I lend you ten pounds and you don't thank me. A simple thanks as in (30) would be lower on the politeness scale than something like (31) which involves features designed to make the utterance more polite:

(30) Thanks.
(31) Thank you so much. I really appreciate it. I'll definitely pay you back on Saturday.

Arguably, withheld politeness (not thanking me here) is less polite than either of these. However, there are questions here about how salient the withheld politeness and the other strategies are.

There are, of course, other possibilities which we can understand as more or less polite, e.g. (32) and (33) would be seen as falling between (30) and (31) in terms of how polite they are:

(32) Great, thanks.
(33) That's great. Thank you.

Finally, there are what Culpeper calls '**impoliteness meta-strategies: sarcasm or mock politeness**'. These involve using politeness strategies which are obviously insincere. As with all irony, one way to make clear that you are being ironic is to produce an utterance where a particular feature is more salient than it would usually be. These could be, for example, particular kinds of pitch movements or the use of particular words. Both of these can help to make clear an intention to be impolite. Consider, for example (34) (with or without exaggerated pitch movements):

(34) Thank you so much. I do appreciate this. You are so kind.

As always, of course, the details of the context affect interpretations, including how likely it is that this utterance will seem ironic and rude. This form of words is associated with the possibility of implicated impoliteness, and 'stylised' or exaggerated pitch movements will make this interpretation more likely.

A question to ask about mock impoliteness is whether we need to establish this as a separate strategy or whether we can simply treat this as one place where we can be ironic. We could ask similar questions about the choice of whether to communicate politeness or impoliteness on record or off record and whether to include features which affect the salience or 'weight' of features of politeness.

THREE 'WAVES' OF (IM)POLITENESS THEORIES

There are now many approaches to accounting for politeness phenomena. It is one of the most researched areas in pragmatics and research on this continues to grow. Some researchers identify three 'waves' of research in this area, although there is overlap in that some work thought of as belonging to the first wave includes ideas associated with the second wave, and so on.

The first wave is identified with Brown and Levinson's approach, which claims to be universalist in making claims about 'facework' which apply across cultures and focusing on more general principles rather than personal or idiosyncratic ones. This work focused mainly on politeness strategies which aimed to reduce the force of, or 'mitigate', face-threatening acts.

The second wave grew from criticisms of Brown and Levinson's approach (and some others) which were seen as being based on assumptions about generally Western cultures and were not in fact applicable universally (this is at least a bit unfair since Brown and Levinson based their ideas on research with different cultural groups). Theorists adopting this view also suggested that the focus had been too much on individual utterances (or a small number of utterances in an exchange) rather than on how understanding develops throughout interactions. In this wave, the focus moved more towards the details of specific interactions and on how understanding is constructed dynamically by the interaction of communicators.

Another development at this stage was increased focus on how participants viewed exchanges rather than on how theorists view them.

Researchers expressing this view argued that a mismatch between the ideas developed in theoretical work and the views of participants in exchanges is particularly problematic here and that the views of participants are what the theoretical work should aim to explain. Among other distinctions, this work identified the terms 'first order' politeness (or 'Politeness 1') to refer to the evaluations and attitudes of participants and 'second order' politeness (or 'Politeness 2') for the views of observers or theorists.

The third wave of politeness theory can be seen as attempting a reconciliation or re-balancing in that it adopts aspects of both the first and second wave, aiming to develop theories which take account of and aim to explain the views of participants. There is a focus on both Politeness 1 and Politeness 2, and an aim that these should complement each other, i.e. that ideas about Politeness 2 should fit with and to some extent help us to understand Politeness 1. So these approaches aim to come up with theoretical claims about politeness and social interaction in general, to explore the perceptions, values, and attitudes of individuals, and to explore how the general ideas are evident in specific interactions.

There are many different kinds of approaches within this third wave, varying in many ways. Some adopt neo-Gricean or post-Gricean theoretical approaches, some focus more on social or cultural aspects, some focus on the details of how evaluations of (im)politeness arise. A wide range of methods are used, including observation of interactions and interviews with participants, as well as theoretical discussion.

There has also been an increased tendency to consider how (im)politeness relates to other aspects of social interaction such as the construction of identity, impression and rapport management, cross-cultural variation, and intercultural communication.

FINDING OUT MORE

Here are some ideas for things you might do to develop understanding of ideas in the chapter and to find out more, followed by some suggested further reading.

YOUR OWN EXAMPLES

As ever, look out for and make notes of any interesting examples you come across and see if you can suggest an account of them with reference to the ideas in this chapter. Here are questions you might ask about particular interactions you focus on:

a. How polite or impolite do they seem to you?
b. Is there any evidence of how polite or impolite they are perceived to be by others (people involved in the interaction or other people)?
c. Can you relate these to ideas in the chapter? For example, is positive or negative face involved? Has a face-threatening act been performed? What strategies have communicators used to reduce or increase face threats?

ADAPTING EXAMPLES

You can find out more by adapting the examples you look at, i.e. by suggesting different things communicators could have said, signed, or written. See if you can think of things that would have made the act more or less polite or impolite. Remember to think about nonverbal as well as verbal behaviour here, e.g. about gestures, facial expressions, body positioning, and so on.

CROSS-CULTURAL VARIATION AND INTERCULTURAL COMMUNICATION

As mentioned in the chapter, these are two things which research on (im)politeness has focused on.

You can explore cross-cultural variation by looking at examples from different cultural contexts and looking at how communicative behaviour varies. These might or might not involve different languages. Speakers of the same language in different places sometimes behave differently with regard to (im)politeness.

Work on intercultural communication also usually involves looking at examples and sometimes asking people involved in the interactions about their perceptions of these. You can get started by looking at examples in previous research or at examples you find yourself.

FURTHER READING

Introductory textbooks (including those mentioned in Chapter 1) typically contain introductions to work on (im)politeness. Here are some other useful places to begin finding out more:

1. Bousfield, Derek. 2008. *Impoliteness in Interaction*. John Benjamins.
2. Culpeper, Jonathan. 2009. Impoliteness: Using and Understanding the Language of Offence. ESRC Project Website Hosted at Lancaster University.   https://www.lancaster.ac.uk/fass/projects/impoliteness/ index.htm
3. Culpeper, Jonathan. 2011. *Impoliteness: Using Language to Cause Offence*. Cambridge University Press.
4. Culpeper, Jonathan, Michael Haugh and Dániel Kádár (eds.) 2017. *The Palgrave Handbook of Linguistic (Im)politeness*. Palgrave Macmillan.
5. Haugh, Michael. 2015. *Im/Politeness Implicatures*. Mouton de Gruyter.
6. Haugh, Michael and Yasuhisa Watanabe. 2017. (Im)politeness theory. In Bernadette Vine (ed.) *Handbook of Language in the Workplace*. Routledge: 65–76.
7. Kádár, Daniel Z. 2017. *Politeness in Pragmatics*. Oxford Research Encyclopedia Online. https://doi.org/10.1093/acrefore/9780199384 655.013.218
8. Kádár, Dániel Z. and Michael Haugh. 2013. *Understanding Politeness*. Cambridge University Press.
9. Leech, Geoffrey. 2014. *The Pragmatics of Politeness*. Oxford University Press.
10. Locher, Miriam. 2004. *Power and Politeness in Action*. Mouton de Gruyter.
11. Spencer-Oatey, Helen and Daniel Kádár. 2021. *Intercultural Politeness: Managing Relations Across Cultures*. Cambridge University Press.
13. Terkourafi, Marina. 2012. Politeness and pragmatics. In K. Allan and K.M. Jaszczolt (eds.) *The Camrbidge Handbook of Pragmatics*. Cambridge University Press: 617–637.
12. Terkourafi, Marina. 2019. Im/politeness: a 21st century appraisal. *Foreign Languages and Their Teaching* 1.6: 1–17. Available at: https://hdl .handle.net/1887/85287
15. Watts, Richard. 2003. *Politeness*. Cambridge University Press.

6

WHAT WORDS CAN DO
SPEECH ACTS

So far, we have looked at approaches to pragmatics which have built on Paul Grice's ideas about principles which govern verbal interaction. In this chapter, we consider another important idea developed by a philosopher who worked alongside Grice at Oxford in the mid-twentieth century: John L. Austin. Austin and Grice shared an interest in questions about the philosophy of language. Austin is usually thought of as an 'ordinary language' philosopher, i.e. as one of a group of philosophers who investigated philosophical questions by considering how language is used in everyday interactions (Grice was also associated with this approach but he moved away from it over the years).

A key thing which Austin did was to develop and explore the notion of 'speech acts', i.e. the idea that when we speak we are doing things and that we can understand verbal interaction better if we focus on the kinds of acts which speech can perform. This chapter begins with a summary of Austin's work on speech acts and then considers questions about what kinds of speech acts there are, how they fit within a distinction between semantics (linguistic meaning) and pragmatics (contextually inferred meaning), and how these ideas can be applied in understanding interactions.

DOING THINGS WITH WORDS

Austin's ideas on speech acts were developed over many years and collected in a 1962 book called *How To Do Things With Words* (the book contains the text of the William James lectures he delivered at Harvard in 1955). Austin began his book by suggesting a distinction between utterances which can be thought of as making statements and those which can be thought of as performing acts. In fact, though, as he explained later in the book, he saw all utterances as performing acts. Making a statement, he argued, is also performing an action.

In his initial discussion, he distinguished utterances like (1), which seems to make a descriptive statement and to be evaluable as true or false, from utterances like (2)–(7) which seem instead to perform an action.

(1) There's a new café on the high street.
(2) I promise I'll pay you back on Monday.
(3) I apologise for the inconvenience.
(4) *(spoken at the altar by a person being married)*
     I do.
(5) *(spoken at the altar by someone performing a marriage service)*
     I pronounce you man and wife.

While (1) states that, or describes the state of affairs that, there's a new café on the high street, (2)–(5) all perform actions. By producing the utterance, the speaker makes something happen. The speaker of (2) makes a promise by saying these words, the speaker of (3) makes an apology, the speaker of (4) commits to being married, and the speaker of (5) creates a married couple.

Austin began by distinguishing what he called **constatives** from **performatives**. He used the term **constative** to be broader than 'statement' or 'description' because '[n]ot all true or false statements are descriptions' (Austin 1962: 3). He used the term **performative** because these utterances perform an action rather than making a true or false statement.

Later in the book, Austin argued that in fact **constatives** also perform an action in that they assert that a proposition is true. Austin's rhetorical tactic in the lectures and the book was to begin with what seemed like a 'common-sense' statement that some utterances make statements while others perform actions and then to move on to argue that all utterances perform actions.

TYPES OF SPEECH ACTS

Alongside his claim that utterances perform actions, Austin made a number of distinctions among speech acts.

First, he pointed out that some expressions are **explicit performatives** in that they contain a verb (a 'performative' verb) which explicitly commits the speaker to performing the act it refers to. Examples include the first-person uses of the verbs *promise*, *apologise*, and *pronounce* in (2), (3), and (5) above. Austin distinguished explicit performatives from what he called 'primary utterances' which do not contain a performative verb. These may still perform an action, of course. Given the right contextual assumptions, I can promise to pay you back by uttering (6):

(6) I'll pay you back on Monday.

Promising in this way is, of course, less certain and less reliable than with the explicit performative in (2). I can more plausibly deny that I promised after having said (6) than if I have explicitly promised as in (2).

As I said above, Austin moved from a distinction between constatives and performatives to the claim that all utterances perform speech acts (he called this move a 'sea change' in his argument but it was one he had planned in advance). So he argues that even constatives perform actions. We'll look at some more specific properties of speech acts below.

A key question which was discussed in developing ideas about speech acts concerned what kinds of speech acts there are. Austin made suggestions on this (which he saw as a tentative starting point), and several other theorists discussed this and suggested different sets. One of the most influential theorists was John R. Searle (a student of Austin's) and so I present one of his ways of categorising speech acts here. Searle suggested slightly different categories in different discussions and also changed some of the terms. My main focus here is on helping you to understand the general idea rather than any specific list of categories. In one of his groupings, he distinguished five categories, each of which he envisaged as having sub-categories. They are:

Representatives, which commit the speaker to something being the case, such as:

(7) The sun has just come out.

Directives, which are attempts by the speaker to get the hearer to do something, such as:

(8) Pass me the salt.

This category also includes questions, which can be understood as requests to provide some information:

(9) What time is the next train due?

Commissives, which commit the speaker to doing something in future, such as:

(10) I promise to be there on time.
(11) I'll be there on time.

Expressives, which indicate an emotional reaction or a psychological state, such as:

(12) What a great performance!
(13) Am I pleased to see you!

Declarations, which change the way the world is so that the state of affairs the words refer to becomes true, such as:

(14) I name this ship Boaty McBoatface.
(15) I declare these games open.

(You can read here about a failed attempt to name a ship *Boaty McBoatface* in 2016: https://en.wikipedia.org/wiki/Boaty_McBoatfac e The name was instead given to an autosub on the ship. Some commentators later coined the term *McBoatfacing* to refer to the act of 'letting the internet decide things').

Searle and others explored a number of properties of the various kinds of speech acts. To take just one example, he suggested that some speech acts can be seen as being about getting the speaker's words to fit the world while others are about getting the world to fit the words. Representatives are about words fitting the world since the words are committing the speaker to the truth of a state of affairs in the world. Promises, on the other hand, are about getting the world to fit the words, since they commit the speaker to making the world be as the words indicate. Declarations, he suggested are both. The speaker's words describe the world (words to world) but they also make the state of affairs they describe true (world to words).

PROPERTIES OF SPEECH ACTS

Austin explored a number of other questions about speech acts. One concerned what he termed the **felicity conditions** for the performance of a speech act, i.e. the conditions which must hold for a particular act to be successfully performed. These have also been the topic of much discussion and there has been some disagreement about them. Here are some examples.

To order somebody to do something (a kind of directive), it seems that the speaker must have some power over the hearer. If the hearer has more power than the speaker, then the order will not succeed. If I am going to promise to do something, it must be within my power to bring it about, I can't, for example, promise to win first prize in a competition I have entered. If I apologise to you, then it seems that I must actually be sorry for what I have done. For this reason, some of these conditions are termed **sincerity conditions**.

There is, of course, room for debate about many of these. There is often disagreement about apologies, for example. Consider some of the debates which arise when a politician uses one of the following forms of words:

(16) I apologise…
(17) I'm sorry…
(18) I regret…

and also how responses vary depending on what comes next, e.g. the difference between these utterances:

(19) I apologise for offending you.
(20) I apologise for any offence I may have inadvertently caused.
(21) I'm sorry if you found my remarks offensive.

Most people think that (20) and (21) are less convincing apologies than (19). It seems that simply saying something like '*I apologise*' is not enough for an apology to have been successfully performed.

Austin also suggested that utterances perform a number of different acts simultaneously. He identified six kinds of acts which utterances perform: **phonetic acts** are the acts of producing sounds; **phatic acts** are the acts of producing words with grammatical form and intonation (Austin does not mention sign languages but of course his ideas apply in the same way to producing signs in a sign language); **rhetic acts** are the acts of producing utterances with a sense and reference (i.e. with a meaning). Arguably the acts which are most important for pragmatics, and the ones which have been most discussed in work on linguistic semantics and pragmatics are **locutionary, illocutionary** and **perlocutionary** acts.

Locutionary acts are seen as the combination of phonetic, phatic, and rhetic acts. They are acts of saying something which consists of words and grammatical forms with a meaning.

Illocutionary acts are central to Austin's and Searle's accounts as they are the acts of performing an action, i.e. of uttering something with a particular 'force'. Stating, requesting, promising, apologising, and so on are illocutionary acts.

Perlocutionary acts are the acts of achieving an effect on the addressee. They are achieved through performing an illocutionary act. So they might include pleasing, irritating, insulting, and so on.

On Austin's view, speech acts are complexes made up of all of these acts performed at once. Consider an utterance of (22), for example, as a response to a request to give up the speaker's seat to someone who has reserved it on a train:

(22) I'm not moving.

The speaker has performed:

(23) Acts performed by an utterance of (22) in a specific context:
   a. The **phonetic act** of producing noises
   b. The **phatic act** of uttering the words '*I'm not moving*' with particular intonation
   c. The **rhetic act** of producing these words with a sense and reference (including using *I* to refer to the speaker and *moving* in the sense of changing position).

d. The **locutionary act** (combining a, b, and c) of saying '*I'm not moving*'.

e. The **illocutionary act** of stating that the speaker is not moving (and indirectly refusing to comply with a request).

f. The **perlocutionary act** of making the hearer angry, offended, etc.

Austin suggested that we need to recognise each of these acts in order to understand verbal communication.

SPEECH ACTS, SEMANTICS, AND PRAGMATICS

Austin's ideas have been very influential and they were also assumed by Grice, who saw speech acts as being performed by utterances, with 'what is said' and 'what is implicated' constituting two speech acts performed at the same time. Others, e.g. Searle, termed these 'direct' and 'indirect' speech acts. An interesting question is how we can relate the distinction between linguistic semantics and pragmatics to Austin's ideas.

SPEECH ACTS IN SEMANTICS

Before Austin proposed the idea of speech acts, much work on linguistic semantics (i.e. the study of linguistically encoded meanings) focused on utterances which make statements, describing things in the world. The most common way of accounting for what they mean was to relate them to the conditions under which what they say would be considered true. This can seem confusing at first and some ways of speaking about it add to the confusion. Part of the idea is that we need to characterise the meanings of linguistic expressions without being circular and just using other expressions to explain them. An analogy is sometimes made with what happens when we look up a word we don't know in a dictionary. Sometimes, the dictionary definition contains another word we don't know. We then need to look that word up. Sometimes, we keep looking up new words until we end up with a definition which includes the word we started with. Imagine for example, if we looked up *bull* and the definition said 'a male cow'. If we don't know what a *cow* is, we might look it up. What if the definition said 'a female bull'? This particular example is not likely but the key point to notice is that we are not really capturing the meaning of an expression if we just define it using other expressions. Defining a word using a different natural language, say translating from English to French, would similarly not explain meanings. When one approach to linguistic meaning (Katz and Fodor's 1963 approach) proposed to account for meanings by assigning semantic 'markers' to words, the philosopher David Lewis suggested that this was a case of translation, into a language he called 'markerese', rather than an explanation of what the original expressions meant. To get out of this problem, semanticists suggested that we could characterise the meaning of an expression by stating the conditions under which it would be true.

There is something intuitive about this. If we know the meaning of an expression and we know relevant facts about the world, we will know whether it is true (strictly speaking, whether it is representing a true proposition). If I understand what *my tyre has a puncture* means and I know whether there is a significant amount of air escaping from my tyre, then I can say whether an utterance of this expression is true. We can extend this by saying that if we know the meaning of something which is not true then we know what the world would have to be like for it to be true, e.g. if I understand the expression *there is a tiger in the garden*, I know what the world would have to be like for an utterance of this expression to represent a true proposition.

One reason that this approach often seems odd is that it's hard to find ways of characterising the truth conditions of an utterance and so semanticists and philosophers have often resorted just to using words in English or another human language and trusting readers to understand that these represent whatever the world would have to be like for them to be true. In a famous example, the philosopher Donald Davidson (1967) suggested characterising the meaning of the expression *snow is white* by saying:

(24) *snow is white* is true if and only if 'snow is white'

To understand this, it's important to see that the inverted commas are there to indicate that this clause represents whatever the truth conditions of *snow is white* are (i.e. what the world would have to be like for *snow is white* to represent a true proposition).

There are many problems with this approach, i.e. with assuming what is usually called a 'truth-conditional semantics'. Some of them follow from the assumption, now dropped by many theorists, that linguistic expressions (even statements) directly represent something which can be evaluated for truth or falsity. One problem which was focused on in work around the time when Austin's ideas were published and discussed, was that many linguistic expressions clearly do not express something which could be true or false. These include the 'non-declarative' sentences in (25)–(28):

(25)   Close the door.
(26)   Is it raining?
(27)   What time is it?
(28)   (Wow!) Am I glad to see you!
(29)   What a fool I am!

We cannot ask whether the speaker of any of these has said something true or not and it would be weird to reply '*that's not true*' to any of them. We might say this after hearing one of them but we would be understood to be contradicting something which follows from the expression rather than what it directly communicates. There are, of course, lots of other examples of expressions which don't make statements and so cannot be analysed by referring to their truth conditions. Our semantic theories will be far from successful if they only apply to statements.

Austin's approach suggests a possible solution. If we consider that utterances can perform a number of kinds of acts, then we might account for their meaning not by considering the conditions under which they would be true but by considering their 'felicity conditions' (which I mentioned above) or conditions under which they would be successfully performed or 'satisfied'. Rather than saying that *close the door* is true under certain conditions, we can say that it is satisfied if the addressee has been requested to close the door.

Some theorists proposed associating particular 'sentence types' with particular illocutionary forces. This approach depends, of course, on us being able to identify a range of sentence types to map onto illocutionary forces, which is not in fact easy to do. Assuming that this is not problematic, though, we might suggest (as some have done) that sentences consist of a 'propositional content' and an illocutionary force (or force potential). The idea would be, for example, that *It's raining*, *Is it raining?*, and *rain!* share propositional content representing the proposition that it rains but differ with regard to what kind of illocutionary force they indicate. We might represent the illocutionary force as F and the propositional content as p and describe the illocutionary force as operating alongside p each time. This idea is sometimes represented by saying that the meaning of a sentence can be understood as $F(p)$, i.e. as the sentence's 'propositional content' along with a force operator. We can then propose semantic analyses like these:

Possible semantic analyses of sentence types:

a. **declaratives** (like *it is raining*):
    perform an **assertive** speech act where the speaker is committing herself to the truth of the propositional content p

b. **imperatives** (like *close the door*):
    perform a **directive** speech act where the speaker is requesting the hearer to bring about the state of affairs represented by p

c. **interrogatives** (like *is it raining?*):
    perform a **directive** speech act where the speaker is requesting the hearer to provide information about the state of affairs represented by p

d. **exclamatives** (like *what a fool I am!*):
    perform an expressive speech act where the speaker expresses surprise at the state of affairs represented by p

On this approach, then, we can maintain a truth-conditional semantics by seeing the (truth-conditional) content of the proposition expressed as embedded within a force indicated by the sentence type. In effect, of course, this means that we have a complex proposition with the central proposition embedded as a sub-part.

The most significant problem with this approach is that it is hard to characterise what the force associated with each sentence type would be. There seem to be counterexamples to all of the claims we might make. There are, for example, declaratives which seem not to commit the speaker to the truth of the proposition expressed:

(30) A man walks into a bar.
(31) Imagine this. You are on a desert island…
(32) It's raining.

(30) could be the opening of a piece of prose fiction or a joke. The second part of (31) is the utterance of a declarative sentence intended to represent an imagined situation. The utterance in (32) has the form of a declarative but in many contexts it can be understood as asking a question rather than making a statement (we can make this interpretation more likely by using particular kinds of prosody or nonverbal behaviour).

There are imperatives which do not seem to request an action, such as the dare in (33), the threat in (34), and the utterance in (35), which seems to be informing us of something (these have been called 'pseudo-imperatives'):

(33) Come one step closer. I dare you!
(34) Do that one more time and I'll throw you out.
(35) Look behind the fridge and you won't believe the mess you find there.

There are interrogatives which do not seem to be asking anybody to inform the speaker of anything, such as the exam question in (36), the encouragement to guess in (37), and the rhetorical question in (38):

(36) What is the Cooperative Principle and how does Grice see its role in communication?
(37) Which hand is the chocolate in?
(38) What do we say before we leave the table?

There is considerable work to do if we are to construct a realistic account of the meanings of different types of sentences by assuming that different forms represent different kinds of speech acts.

SPEECH ACTS IN PRAGMATICS

Given these problems, some semanticists argue that the illocutionary force of utterances is pragmatically inferred so that we work out, for example, whether an utterance of a declarative like (39) or (40) is intended to represent a statement or a question:

(39) You're enjoying this.
(40) We're allowed to interpret the regulation as allowing late submissions.

Both of these could be used either to make a statement or to ask a question, and contextual factors seem to play a role in this. Notice that the form of the utterance affects the likelihood of particular interpretations. Given that the hearer is more likely to know whether they are enjoying something than the speaker, (39) is more likely to be taken as a question than as a statement.

Intonation plays a role here, of course, so that, for example, an utterance of (39) with rising intonation is more likely to be taken as a question than one with falling intonation. We'll look at intonation again in Chapter 7.

As mentioned above, an important notion in speech act theory is the distinction between direct and indirect speech acts. Here is an example:

(41) Adam: Do you want to go for a coffee?
      Bella: I've got to prepare for a seminar.

Bella's direct speech act here is the statement that she has to prepare for a seminar. We have to infer, of course, that the seminar is happening quite soon and that she can't both prepare for the seminar and go for coffee with Adam. Having done that, Adam can infer that she is turning down his invitation. This is an indirect speech act.

Clearly, indirect speech acts are implicatures and one way of thinking about Grice's ideas is to say that he was offering an account of how we infer indirect speech acts.

This notion is important in thinking about (im)politeness. One motivation for performing a speech act indirectly is that it can make a communicative act more polite. Here, Bella avoids implicatures about her not wanting to have coffee with Adam by making a statement which gives a reason for her not being able to accept his invitation.

We can, of course, be impolite indirectly as well. Here is another possible response which Bella could have given to Adam's invitation:

(42) That would mean spending time with you.

Here, Bella's indirectness makes her utterance less polite as Adam needs to infer (at least) two other assumptions: that Bella doesn't want to do things which mean spending time with Adam and then that she is turning down his invitation.

CONVENTIONALISED INDIRECT SPEECH ACTS?

Some indirect speech acts seem to be conventionally associated with particular forms. A classic example is (43), which was discussed by Searle (1975), among others:

(43) Can you pass the salt?

This seems to be asking a question about whether the hearer is able to pass the salt. For Searle, this would be a directive speech act, requesting information. Of course, in most contexts, this would be understood as a request to pass the salt. This is also a directive, but this time it's a request for action rather than information.

As expressions like this are so often used to make requests, it seems possible that this has become conventionalised, i.e. it is now part of the linguistic meaning of the expression. There has been a lot of discussion about exactly how to account for expressions like this. On the one hand, it seems that we routinely assume that an expression such as (43) is asking for the salt to be passed. On the other hand, the expression still has the other sense. We are more likely to take an utterance like (44) as a request for information:

(44) Can you speak Turkish?

However, it is possible to understand (43) as a request for information, e.g. if we ask a young child about a particularly large or heavy salt container. (44) could also be a request to speak Turkish, if for example the speaker speaks Turkish and English and the hearer is struggling to express themself in English.

We can also use other expressions to make requests. I have been asked to do things with each of these forms:

(45) Are you able to do the dishes?
(46) Do you want to give the table a quick wipe?
(47) Is there any way you could help me to make the tea?

Clearly, (im)politeness is also relevant here. As we've seen, speakers sometimes convey things indirectly to avoid the risk of being impolite. These expressions seem to have developed their common indirect meanings after being used frequently for politeness reasons.

A question researchers have asked, and which is still being discussed, is whether these have become fully conventionalised, so that (43), for example, is ambiguous and we need to infer which sense is intended each time or whether these are better treated as pragmatic, either as generalised or particularised conversational implicatures (which we discussed in chapter two).

DO WE ALWAYS NEED TO RECOGNISE SPEECH ACTS?

A final question to ask here is whether we actually need to identify which speech act an utterance has performed in order to understand it. It's possible that we often don't need to do this. We do need to do this for acts which are associated with specific recognised social conventions. For example, when the official in a sports contest announces a decision, this determines what has just happened in the game, e.g. when a tennis umpire says. 'Overruled. The ball was in.' This means that the ball counts as having been in. Anyone who didn't recognise that this is a ruling within the game would not have understood the utterance. It's less clear, though, that we need to categorise every utterance we hear as, for example, a statement or a request. Arguably, what matters is that hearers make inferences which allow them to come up with an interpretation rather than to come up with the right label for an utterance. Consider (48), for example:

(48) Don't take another step.

Arguably, what is important is that the hearer recognises that the speaker wants them to stop moving rather than that they label this as a request.

Similarly, we might ask whether we need to think explicitly about the status of (43) as a request to pass the salt in order to understand it.

APPLYING SPEECH ACT THEORY

Even without answering questions about semantics and pragmatics, we can apply ideas about speech acts in analysing communicative acts. We might, for example, consider what kinds of speech acts an individual chooses to perform in particular situations and consider what effects this has on the interaction.

A therapist, for example, is more likely to ask questions than an aerobics instructor. Teachers can decide what kinds of speech acts are most appropriate in different situations, e.g. deciding whether to order a pupil to do something or to remind them of expected behaviour by asking a rhetorical question:

> (49) Jake! Sit down and be quiet!
> (50) Jake, what do we do when we're getting ready for story time?

We can also apply ideas about speech acts when considering (im) politeness in interactions. As we have seen, a direct request such as (51) threatens the face of both the speaker and hearer. We might, therefore, make a request indirectly as in (52) or produce an utterance like (53) which can be understood as a 'pre-request':

> (51) Give me one of those.
> (52) I'd love to try one of those.
> (53) Are you doing anything tomorrow evening?

The hearer of (53) might respond by saying what they are doing tomorrow night, e.g. as in (54):

> (54) I'm going to visit relatives in Darlington.

If they do, they avoid the risks involved if the speaker asked them for help with something directly as in (55):

> (55) Could you help me with some work I need to do in my garden tomorrow evening?

As we just saw, these ways of communicating seem to lead to some degree of conventionalisation in some cases so that *can you X* is often used to request somebody to do X and, arguably, this has become part of their linguistic meaning.

Focusing on speech acts can help us to understand many cases of linguistic communication and communication strategies. In (56), for example, this notice (on a train) has been formulated in such a way as to express gratitude rather than using something like (57) which makes a direct request or order:

(56) Thank you for not smoking in this carriage.
(57) Do not put your feet on the seats.

Decisions about which speech acts to perform directly seem to be common in lots of verbal communication.

Austin's idea that we perform speech acts when we produce utterances has been very influential. It has been applied in semantics and pragmatics with a range of approaches adopting it in both areas. It has been helpful in considering how we interact in general and also in understanding how we are more less polite or impolite in interactions.

The notion of speech acts has been used to help describe particular kinds of acts and, relatedly, as a useful way to develop understanding of interactions.

FINDING OUT MORE

Here are some ideas for things you might do to develop understanding of ideas in the chapter and to find out more, followed by some suggested further reading.

YOUR OWN EXAMPLES

In looking at your own examples here, you might focus on noting which speech acts you think are being performed in each case, categorising them as direct or indirect speech acts, and thinking about the effects of formulating utterances in this way. Remember to think about how polite or impolite particular utterances are.

ADAPTING EXAMPLES

Again, you can find out more by adapting the examples you look at, i.e. by suggesting different formulations. For this chapter, try choosing different speech acts, e.g. changing a directive speech act which requests action like *don't throw those dishes about like that* to a statement which makes an indirect request such as *those dishes are quite fragile*.

FURTHER READING

Again, there is introductory discussion of speech acts in most introductory textbooks so the books listed at the end of Chapter 1 are useful starting points.

The first main source on speech acts is:

1.	Austin, John L. 1962. *How to Do Things with Words*. Clarendon. (There's also a 2nd edition, edited by J. O. Urmson and Marina Sbisà, which was published in 1975).

John Searle's work has also been influential, including these two books:

2.	Searle, John R. 1969. *Speech Acts: An Essay in the Philosophy of Language*. Cambridge University Press.
3.	Searle, John R. 1979. *Expression and Meaning*. Cambridge University Press.

7

BEYOND WORDS
PROSODY

Early work in pragmatics focused on the interaction of linguistic meanings (the meanings of words and other linguistic expressions) with aspects of the context, explaining how we understand particular utterances with reference to pragmatic principles. More recent work has focused on how meanings develop through interactions and on complexities which were often put aside in early work which often focused on individual utterances. There has been increased interest over the years in how things other than words affect what is communicated, sometimes accompanying words and sometimes in purely nonverbal communication. This chapter discusses prosody, which is about such things as pitch movement, tempo, and volume which are not linguistic but affect how utterances sound. The next chapter discusses nonverbal communication and multimodal communication.

To begin thinking about how things other than words affect communication, consider this utterance which I said to a student in class recently:

(1) That is a very good point.

A discussion of this example which focused mainly on linguistic forms (e.g. Grice's approach) might aim to account for it by identifying something like what is represented in (2):

(2) *Contextual assumptions*:
A student has just said something about the topic we are discussing.
What is directly communicated ('said' or explicature):
What the student said is a very good point.
Implicatures:
The student's contribution is important.
The student has helped develop the discussion in a useful way.

This probably seems like a reasonable account of what happened. However, I have missed out some important features of the conversation. I have kept the context minimal as that does not affect the discussion here. There are several other things which affect the interpretation quite significantly.

First, I stressed the words *that* and *very*. I could represent this stress placement as follows:

(3) THAT is a VERY good point.

I also paused after *that* so that my utterance consisted of two units. I could represent the pause with a full stop in brackets and represent it as follows:

(4) THAT (.) is a VERY good point.

The volume of my speech was louder on *that* and *very* and my pitch fell from a fairly high position. Following a convention where I use \ to represent a falling tone and / to represent a rising tone, without distinguishing lower and higher examples of each, I could represent this as follows:

(5) \ THAT (.) is a \ VERY good point

My utterance would have been understood differently if I had said it fairly quickly, as one unit, and with a low fall on *point* (making it likely that I would contract *is* as follows):

(6) That's a very good \ POINT

There are, of course, other places where I could have placed the stress and other pitch patterns I could have used. These are all features of **prosody**.

I also did some **nonverbal** things which were relevant here. I pointed my finger in the direction of the student throughout my utterance and brought my hand up and down when saying the two words I stressed. At those same moments, my eyes opened wider and my eyebrows went up.

It was also relevant that there were words on a whiteboard behind me while I was speaking. Some of these were written by students and some by me. I did not point to them at this moment but I did when producing other utterances during the class. This means that we were engaging in **multimodal communication**. Of course, my utterance itself was multimodal, given that I moved parts of my body (I mentioned my hands, eyes, and eyebrows above) while talking and this contributed to how my utterance was understood.

I could have mentioned lots of other things here, including other aspects of my voice, images I projected at some points during the class, other ways in which I and the students moved our bodies (my stance and how I moved around the room, sometimes sitting with students while we discussed things and sometimes crouching down near where they were sitting). This chapter discusses some of the nonverbal things which affect communication, focusing in turn on prosody, nonverbal communication, and multimodal communication.

PROSODIC FORMS

Prosody is a term used to cover various aspects of how linguistic expressions are produced other than the fact that particular speech sounds or signs have been uttered. So, for example, an utterance of *that's a good point*, (a shorter version of the example above) could be uttered with rising / or falling \ intonation, and with one or more stresses on different syllables, as in (7)–(10):

(7) That's a \ GOOD point.
(8) That's a / GOOD point.
(9) \ THAT'S a good point.
(10) \ THAT'S a \ GOOD \ POINT.

In each case, the hearer will recognise that the same expressions have been uttered but differences in stress placement and pitch movement affect how the utterance is understood.

In linguistics, speech sounds which play a role in a linguistic system are called 'phonemes' and are usually represented in slanted brackets. One way to identify a phoneme is to see that it can be used in place of another phoneme to distinguish two different words. For example, we can see that /p/ (a sound made by pushing air into the mouth with our lips together and releasing air quite forcefully when the lips come apart) is a phoneme in English because it distinguishes the word *pip,* represented phonemically as /p ɪ p/, from *dip, hip, lip, sip,* and other words.

Prosody is about aspects of sounds other than those involved in producing the phonemes. These include pitch level and movement (intonation), volume, stress (which can be indicated by pitch placement and volume), rhythm, and voice quality. We can see that these do not contribute to phonemes as we can say a word like *pip* with higher or lower pitch, in a whisper or creaky voice, louder or quieter, faster or slower, and so on, without changing our perception of the word as *pip.*

STRESS PLACEMENT

It's clear that prosodic features can affect how we understand particular utterances, e.g. the placement of fairly prominent stress (often termed 'contrastive') in (12)–(15) affects how we understand the utterances:

> (11) CALUM didn't eat my chocolates
> (12) Calum didn't EAT my chocolates
> (13) Calum didn't eat MY chocolates
> (14) Calum didn't eat my CHOCOLATES

(11) is likely to be taken to suggest that somebody other than Calum ate my chocolates, (12) that Calum did something to my chocolates other than eating them, (13) that Calum ate somebody's chocolates but not mine, and (14) that Calum ate something of mine other than my chocolates.

A well-known example used to illustrate the effects of stress placement is the contrast between (15) and (16):

(15) I'm sorry I'm late. My father was ill and I had to feed the PIG.

(16) I'm sorry I'm late. My father was ill and I had to FEED the pig.

In (15) we are likely to assume that the pig and the father are not the same entity while in (16) we are likely to think that they are.

INTONATION

Pitch movement and placement ('intonation') can also affect meanings. In some languages, called **tone languages**, different tones on a syllable represent different linguistic meanings. For example, in northern Vietnamese varieties the sequence of sounds /b a/ has a different meaning depending on what tone it is associated with, as follows:

meanings of /b a/ with different tones in northern Vietnamese varieties:

mid level:	'three'
low falling (breathy):	'lady', 'grandmother' (and several other meanings)
mid rising, tense:	'father's elder brother' (and some other meanings)
mid falling, glottalised, short:	'at random', 'any' (as in *anymore*), with negative connotations, e.g. in complaints, or suggesting thoughtlessness (e.g. that somebody will ask anyone something without considering consequences)
mid falling(-rising), harsh:	'poison'
mid rising, glottalised:	'residue'

In non-tone languages, like English, intonation is used not to indicate linguistic meanings but for other purposes. For example, some intonation patterns are likely to suggest that the speaker is asking a question, others that she finds something surprising, and others that she is being ironic. It is hard to pin these down, and there are variations among different varieties of English, so it is hard to provide clear examples. In some contexts, a high rising tone on (17) is likely to sound like the speaker is asking a question:

(17) Calum / likes the book

This tone is also often used when making a statement, including when telling others about a series of events.

A fall-rise (where pitch falls and then rises again) is likely to be taken to suggest that the speaker has more to say:

(18) Calum ∨ likes the book

If so, we might expect the speaker to go on to say something like (19) or (20) (there are other possibilities, of course):

(19) He doesn't love it, though.
(20) But not enough to suggest it for his book club.

Or the speaker might not say anything more and leave it to the hearer to make inferences about what more she might intend (these would be relatively weak implicatures, of course).

It is hard to account for all of the effects of prosody. For tone languages, it is clear that the tones are part of language and contribute to linguistic meaning. In languages like English, there is debate about whether we should treat prosody as semantic or pragmatic. One reason for seeing prosody as semantic is that some aspects of it vary according to the speaker's dialect, e.g. speakers of some varieties in Belfast, Glasgow, Newcastle, and Liverpool typically produce statements with a low rise while speakers of other varieties are likely to produce these with a falling tone. The ways that context interacts with prosody make it seem pragmatic. For example, a rising tone accompanying (21) is likely to suggest that the speaker is asking a question but the speaker can also ask a question with a falling tone here:

(21) You're enjoying this book.

A significant difference between (21) and (17), which we looked at above, is that we would usually assume that the hearer of (21) is in a better position than the speaker to know whether they are enjoying the book. For (17), there is no reason (without further contextual assumptions) to think that either the speaker or the hearer has more insight into whether Calum likes the book. This is one possible reason why we are more likely to ask a question with a falling tone when saying (21) than (17), and also evidence for the role of pragmatics in understanding prosody.

There is arguably a third kind of language, called a 'pitch-accent language', where the placing of pitch-accents (which make particular syllables prominent) differentiates words (languages which have been described as pitch-accent languages include Basque, Japanese, Norwegian, Slovene, and Turkish). Arguably, English has a very small amount of this feature but only for words such as *record* and *rebel* where the noun version has an accent on the first syllable while the verb has an accent on the second syllable.

As we are interested in pragmatics rather than the linguistic system here, we will not say more about the use of prosody to identify words in tone and pitch-accent languages.

All languages have prosody, including sign languages. Sign languages share all the properties of spoken languages apart from the use of sounds produced by the control of airflow from the diaphragm up through the body and out through the nose or mouth. Sign languages have phonemes, morphemes, words, phrases, and clauses just as spoken languages do. They also have prosodic features, i.e. things which affect understanding without contributing to the production or perception of phonemes. In sign languages, prosodic features include such things as the duration of a sign, pauses, facial expressions, how open the eyes are, and the use of the signing space. So the questions we ask about prosody affect sign languages too.

WHAT DO PROSODIC FORMS MEAN?

While there has been much discussion of the meaning of prosody, there is not at this stage clear agreement on its nature or how it works, with disagreements about whether it is linguistic or non-linguistic, whether it gives rise to 'encoded' meanings (which may not be linguistic) or whether it functions more like a 'natural highlighting' device (similar to pointing), and so on. Accounting for prosody is made harder by differences among varieties (whether or not we describe such varieties as different languages or different varieties of the same language), and the considerable variation among speakers, with even individuals varying the ways they realise utterances in different contexts.

There are also different ways of representing prosody, with some more 'analogue' in the sense that they represent different forms as located on a kind of continuous spectrum and others more 'digital' in that they identify different categories (while understanding that the physical, i.e. acoustic, properties are continuously related). It's hard to be confident that it makes sense to represent things categorically, e.g. as 'high' versus 'low' tones. Consider, for example, an utterance of *I'm tired* with a fairly typical falling tone. The pitch of the utterance might start fairly high and end fairly low. It might start by going up slightly before it goes down. Every speaker has a different pitch range and individual speakers change their pitch range, sometimes intentionally for effect and sometimes not. Despite all of this variation, many representations simply indicate that each of these would count as a falling tone. One way of representing this is simply to have a falling slanted line before the 'pitch accent', i.e. the syllable associated with the intonational form:

(22) I'm \ tired.

This is simplifying significantly and leaves much for the person reading the representation to infer. All that we know from this is that the pitch mainly falls overall. This system is often associated with one (O'Connor and Arnold 1961 is one influential source which uses this system, for example) which assumes English has five tone contours: FALL, RISE, RISE-FALL, FALL-RISE, and LEVEL. Each of these can occur more or less high or low and with more or less movement from one pitch to another.

Another system involves writing the words so that they iconically represent the pitch movement, e.g.:

```
                    i
              t     r
                  e
(23) I ' m              d
```

A commonly used system now is called ToBI, which stands for 'Tones and Break Indices'. It was developed by a number of researchers on US English who variously collaborated in the early 1990s (Silverman et al 1992; Beckman and Hirschberg 1994; Pitrelli et al 1994). It was then adopted and adapted for different languages. Simplifying and putting aside some other aspects of the system here, there are five accents which can be associated with an accented word: H, L, L+H*, L*+H, and H+!H*. The star * indicates the primary stress of a word. As well as indicating pitch accents, the system also represents phrase accents and boundary tones. As well as this, a ToBI representation usually includes other information including a representation of the wave form of the utterance. A falling pitch pattern, as I am imagining for the utterance of *I'm tired* here, would have a high pitch accent, indicated by H*, a low phrase accent, represented as L-, and a low boundary tone, represented by L%. So it would look like this:

(24)   Part of a ToBI representation of *I'm tired* with a falling intonation pattern:
H* L- L%

We won't get into the details of the representation of prosody more than this here but it's important to see that representations simplify things and do not represent every aspect of prosodic forms.

While there is ongoing discussion about how prosody affects interpretation, including about what kinds of meanings it conveys and what exactly particular prosodic features do, we have made progress in understanding some things prosody can do and we have developed (partly competing) accounts of how it does these. There are at least three ways in which we might characterise the meanings of prosodic forms. First, they might be part of a linguistic system with encoded meanings similar to morphemes, i.e. they might 'mean something' in a similar way to how the word *chip* is linked to one of several concepts (a deep fried part of a potato, a token used to bet with, a small piece of wood, and so on) or how the {PLURAL} morpheme marks plurality in the words *chips*, *potatoes*, and *wedges*. Second, they might have vaguer meanings like the words *moreover* or the modal verb *could*. Third, they could not have encoded meanings at all but just give rise to meanings because they do something noticeable that makes addressees infer that speakers must intend something by using them, i.e. they could be seen as similar to when a speaker repeats a phrase several times or when somebody rustles a piece of paper to help somebody else guess the right answer in a party game.

IS STRESS A HIGHLIGHTING DEVICE?

Grice made some interesting comments on stress, considering whether we might think of it as a 'natural' highlighting device (which would make it fall into the third kind of category just mentioned) or whether there is evidence that it has become a 'conventionalised' highlighting device, which would mean it falls into the second category just mentioned. He said:

> We might start by trying to think of stress as a purely natural way of high-lighting, or making prominent, a particular word; one might compare putting some object (such as a new hat) in an obvious place in a room so that someone coming into the room will notice or pay attention to it.
>
> (Grice 1989: 50)

He worried that this was not strong enough given that we could also do things like speak in a squeaky voice to highlight things, which suggests that stress is qualitatively different. He went on to consider some more evidence and decided that there is not enough evidence to treat stress as a conventionalised highlighter.

Another view would see stress as a natural highlighter without conventionalised meanings. This would apply to many uses of stress in English (exceptions would be cases where stress position indicates whether a word is a noun or a verb, such as *record* and *rebel*, which we mentioned earlier).

So how could we account for the effects of stress by assuming it is a natural highlighting device? Imagine that we are playing a game and you need to guess which of a number of things I say is the correct answer. As I say one of the words, a person behind me raises an arm and shakes his hand behind my head. There is no coded meaning for what he is doing but you might guess that he is trying to tell you that this is the right answer. He could just as easily have waved a hanky or rolled his head around. Anything he did that is different from what he is doing the rest of the time would highlight that moment and help you to infer that he is indicating the right answer. The fact that almost anything would work is what Grice means in his quote when he points out that there are many things we could use as 'natural highlighting devices'. Pragmatic principles would guide you in making inferences to understand this.

Notice that, for many theorists, the inferences you make when you assume that someone is intending to communicate are different from ones you would make if you did not think so. For relevance theorists, a different principle expresses a generalisation about communicative behaviour from the one which is about cognition in general. For neo-Griceans, assumptions about things like informativeness only apply to communicative behaviour.

Here is an example which looks like it can be explained on the assumption that stress is a natural highlighter:

(25) CALUM didn't eat your chocolates

The stress on Calum here draws attention to that word, suggesting it is more important than other words in the utterance. One reason that this seems plausible is that this is about a contrast between Calum and somebody else who could have been the eater of the chocolates.

There are, however, approaches which suggest that there is something more than 'natural' meaning involved here. Pierrehumbert and Hirschberg (1990), for example, suggest that what ToBI would describe as H* accents (not exactly the same as stress, in fact) are associated with 'new' information. If so, then the stress on *Calum* in (25) would suggest that the idea that Calum ate them is new while the content of the rest of the utterance isn't. It's plausible, then, to suggest that the important thing here is the reference to Calum and that the eating of the chocolates is less important. This doesn't account for the contribution of the negative marker *n't* but we still might say something about stress indicating what's important.

It's not easy to decide between the 'natural highlighting' and 'indicating newness' accounts here but we can begin to explain utterances like (25) if we assume one or the other function for stress.

We could add to the story a notion of 'default' stress (where 'default' suggests a kind of expected or 'unmarked' kind of stress placement). The notion of defaults is also controversial, but it does seem that there are places where stress is more likely to occur in an utterance and that this is affected by assumptions about what is already assumed ('given') and what is 'new'. This is easiest to see in a very short one-clause utterance:

(26) It's RAINing.

The most likely place for the stress here is on the first syllable of *raining*. In this particular case, putting the stress anywhere else (on either *It's* or the second syllable of *raining*) would sound odd. What about a longer utterance like (27)?

(27) John drove to Birmingham yesterday.

A typical utterance here would stress each of *John*, the first syllable of *Birmingham*, and the first syllable of *yesterday*. Putting more prominent stress on one of these adjusts the likely interpretation. Some theorists (e.g. Pierrehumbert and Hirschberg 1990) suggest that this indicates 'new' material (as opposed to 'given'). In this context, 'new' is understood to refer to assumptions being added to what is often referred to as the 'common ground', which we might think of as the set of shared assumptions. A new assumption is one that is being added to the common ground. The term 'given' refers to what the interlocutors already share (and assume that they share). Let's see how this would apply to the following three locations of most prominent stress:

(28) JOHN drove to Birmingham yesterday.
(29) John DROVE to Birmingham yesterday.
(30) John drove to BIRMingham yesterday.

(28) suggests that the speaker is treating the assumption that it was John who drove to Birmingham as new and the idea that somebody drove to Birmingham as given. (29) suggests that John's going to Birmingham was given and the fact that he drove is new. And so on.

There have been several suggestions for how to handle the details of differing stress placements. Intuitions about the effects of different placements are fairly clear for speakers of the same varieties of English.

It is interesting to consider the pragmatic effects of unexpected stress placements. A famous pair of examples is:

(31) He threw a brick against the window and it BROKE.
(32) He threw a brick against the window and IT broke.

(31) seems to suggest that what happened is what we would be likely to expect when a brick hits a window, i.e. that the window broke. (32), by contrast, seems to many speakers to suggest that the brick broke, which is very much not what we would usually expect.

There is a natural way to explain this with reference to pragmatic principles. Given the marked nature of the stress placement in (32), we will assume that there is a reason for this. Hearers will wonder what the unusual thing could be and the idea that *it* has a different referent is fairly accessible and would make sense. There's no sense, of course, in which the referent of *it* (the brick) is new here.

Similarly, the use of what is usually called 'contrastive stress' seems to be something we can explain with reference to pragmatic principles:

(33) John didn't eat your CHOColates.
(34) John didn't EAT your chocolates.

(33) suggests that John might have eaten something else but not the hearer's chocolates while (34) suggests that he might have done something to the chocolates other than eating them. Given that the first syllable of *chocolates* is the most likely place for stress to occur here, the contrastive reading becomes likely when the stress is more clearly marked than we might otherwise expect. The most likely ways to achieve this are to say it more loudly, with higher pitch, or both.

PROSODY AND DISAMBIGUATION

Prosodic form can also help to disambiguate utterances which are associated with more than one linguistic form. (Putting aside the examples mentioned above where stress placement differentiates noun and verb forms of words like *record* and *rebel*).

Prosodic boundaries can help to disambiguate utterances which can be associated with more than one syntactic structure (we looked at some examples of these in Chapter 1), such as:

(35) Calum ate the chocolates in the fridge.
(36) My PhD student who's working on prosody is about to submit.

(35) is syntactically ambiguous between a reading where Calum was in the fridge when he ate the chocolates and one where the

chocolates referred to are the ones that were in the fridge (with no assumption about where Calum ate them). (36) could be intended to identify a specific one of my PhD students, with the assumption being that I have more than one, or it could be referring to my one and only PhD student and, in parenthesis, telling you that she's working on prosody. We can represent the two structures for each in different ways, including tree diagrams and by bracketing. There are different ways to represent the details of the structures. One way is to use a tree diagram. Figure 7.1 presents simplified diagrams to represent two structures for (35).

These are called tree diagrams because they look like upside-down trees with the narrowest part of the diagram (the 'roots' or 'trunk') at the top and branches growing and spreading downwards. The key thing to notice for our purposes here is that all of the words *the chocolates in the fridge* are grouped under one 'node', labelled as an 'NP' for 'noun phrase', in the first diagram but not in the second. This represents the idea that *the chocolates in the fridge* is treated as one noun phrase unit here functioning as the object of the verb and so representing the thing which Calum ate. In the second diagram, *in the fridge* is a separate unit not collected under one node with *the chocolates* and so is taken to tell us something about the eating or the clause as a whole. This leads to the reading where Calum was in the fridge while eating. (There are lots of different ways of representing structures. This is just one option and very much simplified just so we can understand that there are different possible structures here.)

While there are ways of saying both (35) and (36) which don't help to make clear which sense is intended, there are ways which do point in one direction or the other. We can, for example, divide the utterances up into more than one intonation phrase in ways that help to make this clear. **Tonality** is the term used to describe how utterances are split into intonational phrases. The boundaries between phrases are marked with a vertical line: ' | '. We could produce the following utterance with several different divisions into intonational phrases, with some divisions seeming more natural than others. The first one here has no vertical line to indicate that it is treated as one intonational phrase:

(37) Adam hasn't seen Bella performing.
(38) Adam | hasn't seen Bella performing.
(39) Adam hasn't | seen Bella performing.

(40) Adam hasn't seen | Bella performing.
(41) Adam | hasn't seen | Bella performing.

(a)

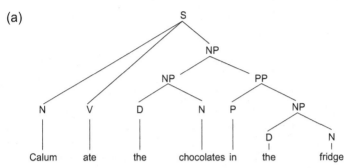

(This structure suggests that it was 'the chocolates in the fridge' which Calum ate but does not say anything about where he ate them)

(b)

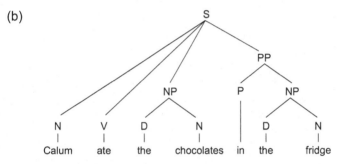

(This structure suggests that Calum was in the fridge when he ate the chocolates)

S = sentence; D = determiner; PP = prepositional phrase;
P = preposition; NP = noun phrase; N = noun; V = verb

FIGURE 7.1 Two syntactic tree diagrams for *Calum ate the chocolates in the fridge.*

These different phrasings affect communication (quite subtly here) but they do not affect how we understand the syntactic structure.

If we say (35) and (36) as one intonational phrase, then that is consistent with either reading of the utterance (with either assumed syntactic structure). We can, though, divide the utterances up in ways which favour one structure over another:

(42) Calum ate | the chocolates in the fridge.
(43) Calum ate the chocolates | in the fridge.
(44) My PhD student who's working on prosody | is about to submit.
(45) My PhD student | who's working on prosody | is about to submit.

(42) suggests that Calum ate the chocolates that had been in the fridge without indicating where he was when he ate them. (43) suggests that Calum was in the fridge at the time of eating.

(44) suggests that the speaker has more than one PhD student and intends here to refer to one who's working on prosody (and that only one of them is working on prosody). (45) suggests that the speaker has exactly one PhD student and is mentioning in passing that the student is working on prosody.

PROSODY AND SPEECH ACTS

We saw in Chapter 6 that there are different ways of thinking about the relationships between sentence structures and meanings. For now, we'll assume the idea that utterances perform speech acts and show how we can think of different prosodic forms, here pitch patterns, as affecting interpretations.

There is a common assumption that utterances in English which would have been seen as making statements (performing 'representative' speech acts) can instead be understood as asking questions (performing 'directive' speech acts requesting information) if they are associated with rising pitch:

(46) You're going to \ Scotland
(47) You're going to / Scotland

On this view, (46), with falling pitch, would be likely to be seen as stating that the referent of *you* is going to Scotland while (47), with rising pitch, would be likely to be seen as asking whether the referent of *you* is going to Scotland. There is something in this idea, and there are contexts where this seems to work, but things are not so simple.

First, it is possible to produce (46), with falling pitch, and be understood to be asking a question. The likelihood of particular interpretations is, of course, affected by the context. Nonverbal behaviour can also affect things. For example, if I point a finger at you while saying (46) and furrow my brow to indicate uncertainty then I am likely to be understood as asking a question.

The effects of pitch are also affected by other linguistic forms. Including *so* at the start or *then* at the end of an utterance (or both) would make it seem more like a question:

(48) So you're going to Scotland.
(49) You're going to Scotland then.

Another complicating factor is that the way we use pitch patterns varies. In some varieties, a low rise here would be a typical way to make a statement. UK places where some speakers do this include Belfast, Glasgow, Liverpool, and Newcastle (where I am writing this).

For varieties of English where a rise is a kind of 'default' statement tone, the rise will be a low one. There are some speakers, though, who use high rising tones when making statements. This phenomenon is sometimes described as 'uptalk'. For speakers who do it, some kinds of utterances are more likely to have rising tones than others. One such situation is when a speaker is telling a story.

IDENTIFYING ATTITUDES

Another way in which intonation is used is to indicate attitudes to what the speaker is saying. In fact, some theorists (including me!) have suggested that particular intonation patterns are associated with particular kinds of attitudes to the proposition expressed and have suggested that this is what leads to different assumptions about speech acts. On this account, attitudes are sometimes taken quite broadly and abstractly, e.g. to include notions such as indicating that the speaker would like to be able to entertain an assumption (and not necessarily a 'propositional form' of the utterance). Rising pitch on (48), for example, would indicate that the speaker would like to be entertaining an assumption. In this case, the hearer would infer that the speaker would like to be thinking that the hearer is going to Scotland (if that is true).

Prosodic forms can also indicate different kinds of attitudes, e.g. amazement or surprise if the speaker uses a marked high rise and fall as in (50):

(50) Calum has finished his essay on ∧ time!

Pitch patterns have also been associated with irony. A common assumption has been that we can distinguish three kinds of intonation pattern we might use when producing an utterance with declarative syntax: 'default' intonation, where there is some rising and falling, 'stylised' intonation, where the rises and falls are more extreme, and 'flat', or 'deadpan', intonation where the rises and falls are less extreme. Consider (51):

(51) Well that's a really good idea.

'Default' intonation would maybe start with a mid-range pitch (relative to how the speaker usually speaks) maintained until the speaker reaches *good* where pitch would rise a little before falling. 'Stylised' intonation would involve sharper and larger rises and falls, e.g. rising sharply on *really* and maintaining that height before falling on the second syllable of *idea*. 'Flat' or 'deadpan' intonation would involve speaking with a fairly low pitch and hardly rising or falling at all.

Some theorists refer to the stylised forms as 'ironic tone of voice'. However, this cannot really be right as it is possible to use them without being taken as ironic. The hearer might, for example, decide that the speaker of an utterance with 'stylised' prosody is just very enthusiastic. Relatively flat or 'deadpan' intonation is also associated with irony but again it is possible to use this without being taken as ironic. This intonation is often used when the speaker and hearer are very close, understand each other well, and do not feel that they need to help each other much with intonational cues to guide interpretations.

We have only scratched the surface here and there is lots of ongoing discussion about how prosody works. Three things are clear. First, prosodic forms help to guide interpretations. Second, prosodic cues interact with contextual assumptions and other forms to help guide interpretations. Finally, we are making progress in understanding how prosody helps us to understand each other (and I am sure we will develop further and fuller accounts of this as research continues).

FINDING OUT MORE

Here are some ideas for things you might do to develop understanding of ideas in the chapter and to find out more, followed by some suggested further reading.

YOUR OWN EXAMPLES

In looking for and making notes of examples here, you might focus on how understanding is affected by prosodic forms.

ADAPTING EXAMPLES

Again, you can find out more by adapting the examples you look at, i.e. by suggesting different formulations. For this chapter, try changing the prosodic forms of utterances and/or changing the linguistic expressions for the same prosodic forms. How do different forms lead to different meanings and how does the same prosody contribute to utterances of different expressions?

FURTHER READING

Prosody is not discussed in all pragmatics textbooks (although I think it should be). Here are two initial readings on prosody (one of which covers nonverbal communication more broadly):

1. Hirschberg, Julia. 2017. Pragmatics and prosody. In Yan Huang (ed.) *Oxford Handbook of Pragmatics*. Oxford University Press: 532–550.
2. Wharton, Tim. 2009. *Pragmatics and Nonverbal Communication*. Cambridge University Press.

BEYOND WORDS
NONVERBAL AND MULTIMODAL COMMUNICATION

The last chapter considered one way in which things other than words can affect communication: prosody. This chapter considers nonverbal communication, with or without accompanying verbal communication, and multimodal communication, i.e. cases where communication involves more than one 'mode'. While a natural assumption might be that speech, writing, and images are three modes, it's not quite that simple and there are different views on what modes there are. We can definitely agree, though, that communication which includes both visual and verbal material is multimodal.

NONVERBAL COMMUNICATION

Work on nonverbal communication raises a similar range of questions. It is usually but not always easy to identify which kinds of acts count as nonverbal and which are verbal. We can easily see that spoken, written, or signed words and larger expressions are linguistic and we can usually recognise which of various kinds of bodily movements and sounds are non-linguistic, e.g. an exaggerated slouching movement or a sigh. It's also clear that some things which begin as nonverbal can be adopted into linguistic systems. The word *yuck*, for example, seems to have emerged from behaviours which mimic the act of throwing up or retching through forms like *eeurgh* and *ugh* to, eventually, *yuck*. We can see that this has become part of a linguistic system as the word can now take morphemes which change its status to that of an adjective, as in *yucky*, and comparative forms like *yuckier*. (There is discussion of cases like this in Wharton 2003, 2009.) Other examples include the move from an ostensive throat clearing to *ahem* and from a clicking noise made with the tongue behind or touching teeth to forms like *tsk* and *tut*. It's not always clear, though, which nonverbal behaviours have conventionalised meanings and which do not.

ANIMAL AND HUMAN COMMUNICATION

Some theorists interested in both verbal and nonverbal communication have looked at the systems used by animals and compared these with types of human communication. An influential approach was developed by Hockett (1960, 1966) who considered what were the 'design features' of human language and compared them with animal communication systems. The conclusion usually drawn from this is that there are animal communication systems which share some properties of human language but none which share them all. Birds, for example, put notes together into songs as we put sounds (phonemes) together into morphemes, words, and utterances containing combinations of these. Vervet monkeys have calls associated with particular meanings, e.g. different cries associated with different predators. Bees can communicate about things which are not immediately present, as their dances make it possible for other bees to locate honey they have found away from the hive. There seem to be examples of most of Hockett's design features in animal communication systems but none have all of them.

Discussion of these questions is ongoing. One suggestion, made by Hauser, Chomsky and Fitch (2002; see also Berwick and Chomsky 2016) among others, is that **recursion** is an essential feature of human language. Roughly, recursion is the property of expressions of a particular category containing other instances of the same category. For example, this expression has clauses embedded inside other clauses:

(1) Adam thought that Bella said that Calum knew that it was raining.

Here *it was raining* is embedded within the clause *Calum knew that it was raining*, which is in turn embedded within *Bella said that...*, which is embedded within *Adam thought that...* There is some evidence that humans use recursion in ways not shared by other species. One view is that we think recursively and that this then plays a role in the nature of human language.

The claim that recursion is a definitional property of human languages is disputed. One argument against this comes Dan Everett (2005, 2008), who claims that the Pirahã language, spoken in Brazil, shows no evidence of recursion. There has been much discussion of this and the debate about this is ongoing.

NATURAL AND NON-NATURAL MEANING

Work on the pragmatics of nonverbal communication has built on Grice's distinction between '**natural**' and '**non-natural meaning**', which we looked at in Chapter 2. Discussion of this can be quite complicated but a simplified version would say that natural meaning does not depend on recognising an intention to communicate while non-natural meaning does.

A classic example of natural meaning is the idea that smoke 'means' fire. If I see smoke in the distance, I can infer that there is a fire because of what I know about the world and, in particular, because I know that smoke is caused by fire.

Non-natural meaning, by contrast, depends on the recognition of an intention to communicate. A typical example discussed in the literature might be somebody who has been asked how their holiday went responding by showing a leg in plaster. Anybody seeing the plaster can infer that the leg in plaster is broken (natural meaning) but inferences about the holiday experience of the person with the leg in plaster depend on treating the behaviour of showing the leg as intentionally communicative.

Non-natural meaning is important for pragmatics, as the pragmatic principles apply only when an act of intentional communication is recognised. It's clear that we act differently when we recognise intentional communication. Another much-discussed kind of case is coughing. If a stranger on the train I'm on starts coughing loudly now, I will not assume that she or he is communicating with me. I will probably just think that they have a cough. Suppose I am talking at a department meeting about some plans for the department and somebody in the room coughs extremely loudly. I might decide that my colleague is doing this in order to communicate something. If I don't think of something right away, I will wonder what they are trying to communicate and might even ask them what they mean.

Do animals ever do things which communicate non-natural meanings? It seems that they do this only to a limited extent. Dancing bees are not communicating intentionally even though their behaviour signals something to other bees. Also, the other bees are not making inferences about what the dancing intends to communicate. Arguably, some animal behaviour is communicating intentionally but there is no evidence that animals ever produce behaviours whose interpretation depends on another recognising an intention to communicate. Thom Scott-Phillips (2015) is one theorist who has argued that the development of the ability to recognise and communicate intentions is central to the evolution of language and so that pragmatics is central to understanding of language as well as communication.

Coming back to Grice's views on meaning and communication, he distinguishes natural from non-natural communication and then distinguishes conventionalised from non-conventionalised (i.e. con- textually inferred) meanings. Since not all conventionalised mean- ings are linguistic (e.g. nodding your head is conventionally associated with agreeing with something in some, but not all, cultures), we can further subdivide conventionalised meanings into linguistic and non- linguistic meaning, as shown in Figure 8.1.

Given later discussion in pragmatics of the nature of connections between linguistic and non-linguistic meanings (particularly how linguistic communication always includes pragmatics and non- linguistic elements), we might want to adjust this diagram, but Grice's ideas are a good starting point for exploring the nature of nonverbal communication.

In the natural world, one way of characterising things (developed by Hauser 1996) is to draw a distinction between natural **signs** and natural **signals**. Signs provide evidence of things but they have not evolved for this purpose. When chimpanzees make nests, they are doing something in order to provide shelter. A by-product of this is that the nests provide evidence that there are chimpanzees in the vicin- ity. Other animals can respond to this evidence, e.g. by moving away to avoid being preyed on by the chimpanzees. **Signals**, by contrast,

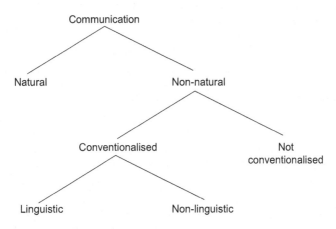

FIGURE 8.1 Grice's types of communication

have evolved in order to communicate something. Bee dances, for example, exist in order to make other bees know where they can find honey. Signals indicate what they do because they evolved for this purpose.

Wharton (2009) discusses this and suggests that human behaviour involves both natural signs and natural signals. He illustrates this by considering shivers and smiles. If someone shivers, then this is a sign that they are cold. Shivering evolved not to communicate but to keep people warm. If someone smiles, by contrast, we know that they are feeling happy or positive. Smiles evolved to communicate this.

However, the distinction between natural and non-natural communication is not clear-cut. We can both shiver and smile more or less ostensively and we can do both in the absence of what they are generally taken to communicate. I can shiver when I am not cold to indicate that I think something is cold or scary, and that thing does not need to be immediately present. I can do this, for example, to communicate that it will be cold when you go somewhere with a cold climate next week or to indicate that I find something we are considering doing scary. Smiles are not always spontaneous responses but sometimes done intentionally to communicate even when we are not actually happy. So both shivers and smiles can be more or less natural in Grice's sense. For some theorists, then (e.g. Sperber and Wilson

1986, 2015; Wharton 2009) communication can be more or less natural in the sense intended by Grice.

When we consider the effects of nonverbal behaviour, it is useful to remember that this can involve natural signs and signals and that these can be more or less natural or non-natural. There are significant differences, for example, between the effects of somebody intentionally producing a shiver in order to communicate ostensively and somebody who can't help themselves from shivering and revealing they are cold even if they intend not to reveal this. Imagine, for example, that you know I've had a cold and you ask me whether I will be OK to cover my teaching this afternoon. I might respond with a stylised fake cough and sneeze and say something like (2):

(2) Oh, don't worry about me. I'll be alright. *(pause)* Probably.

You might see this response as intended to be humorous and assume that I am OK to cover the class.

Suppose that I seem to be masking the fact that my eyes are watering and I am stifling a cough as I say:

(3) No no, don't worry. I'm fine.

You might then decide that I am in fact struggling but that I don't want you to realise that. If you now insist on covering my class for me, then it will be your responsibility and I will not have threatened your face or my own by indicating that I needed help (as discussed in Chapter 5).

Another possibility, reflecting the idea that behaviour can be more or less natural or non-natural, is that I intend for you to notice that I seem ill but I don't want you to see that I intend this. This would count as 'covert' communication. The implications for our relationship are less clear here. You might be fooled, in which case the effects are similar to the case just discussed. On the other hand, you might think that I am intending to communicate covertly and so you might think more negatively of me. There are, of course, several possibilities and you can be more or less confident about whether or not I intended this. It is even possible that I myself am not sure to what extent I was intending to communicate the assumptions about my illness to you.

TYPES OF NONVERBAL COMMUNICATION

What about nonverbal behaviours which definitely count as non-natural communication? We saw examples of this in the discussion of prosody. There are, of course, lots of other ways in which we do this. Among other things, we need to consider things like facial expression, including what our eyes are doing (more or less open or closed? screwed up? blinking?), posture (standing up straight? slouched? relaxed? tense?), and clothes (the difference between wearing jeans and t-shirt or a suit in a workplace or to a party). Research is continuing to develop on all of these.

EMBLEMS, PANTOMIMES, AND BEAT GESTURES

We'll end this section by considering three types of nonverbal action which we can engage in: **emblems**, **pantomimes**, and **beat gestures**. (These ideas were developed, among others, by Alibali et al 2001, Ekman and Friesen 1969, Kendon 1988, 2004, McNeill 1992).

Emblems are culture-specific and have coded meanings. They include (with apologies that some of these are rude and often intended to be offensive) such things as: two fingers raised to mean (in some cultures) 'peace' or something rude (depending on how the hand is presented); a thumb pointing up, which communicates something positive in some cultures and something negative in others; a thumb pointing down, which is negative in some cultures; and a circle made by a thumb and forefinger which means things are good in some cultures and something very rude in others.

As these are coded meanings, they can change just like linguistic meanings. A controversial example in recent years has arisen as extreme right wing and white supremacist groups have used the circle formed by a thumb and forefinger, sometimes called the 'okay' gesture, to indicate affiliation with their views. It has been claimed that this originated in a hoax social media post before becoming used more widely. It has been displayed in courtrooms by people accused of murdering people in a hate crime. An interesting question is what exactly it communicates beyond an expression of membership of the group and so personal and social identity.

Pantomimes are behaviours which do not have coded meanings but which we understand because they resemble what they are representing. These include such things as miming opening a jar or drinking a cup of tea. Pantomimes have the property of being **iconic** in the sense used by Charles Sanders Peirce, the philosopher who played an influential role in early work on semiotics. He distinguished **symbols**, which have conventional meanings (e.g. a red traffic light means 'stop'), **indexes** or **indices** which indicate the presence of something by providing evidence that it is somewhere else (e.g. the presence of smoke indicates that there is fire nearby), and **icons**, which represent things because they resemble them (e.g. a photograph). When we see somebody miming the opening of a jar, we infer that this is what it represents. Of course, these inferences are not fixed so we might not always think the same behaviour represents the same thing. We will also make further inferences based on the pantomimes, just as we do with emblems and verbal utterances. Some pantomimes also become conventionalised to varying degrees.

Beat gestures are movements we make to accompany speech. Metaphorically, we might say they 'punctuate' speech. An example would be when somebody brings their hand down every now and then as they are speaking. Typically, this occurs near a stressed syllable and we can think of these as 'highlighters' in the same way as we might think of some uses of stress in speech. We might for example, bring a hand down, or move a hand away from our body as we utter the words *not* and *no* in this utterance:

(4) I'm NOT doing that. There's NO way!

A full account of how we understand each other, and therefore a full pragmatic theory, will provide an account of what different nonverbal behaviours mean, of what kinds of meanings they have, and of how they interact with other things in communicative behaviour.

MULTIMODAL COMMUNICATION

The notion of '**multimodality**' relates to the idea that we can communicate in more than one '**mode**'. There are different ways of thinking about modes and different terms used by different theorists. Within social semiotics, where much of the ground-breaking work on this was developed (e.g. Kress and van Leeuwen 2010), the term 'semiotic resource' is often used, indicating something we can use to convey meanings. This is helpful, as it makes clearer what kinds of phenomena we are discussing and how to decide what things count as a different semiotic resource rather than a different mode. Kress and van Leeuwen, like many theorists working on this topic, adopt a 'social semiotic' approach with roots in Michael Halliday's functional approach to language which sees forms and functions as unified (rather than thinking of linguistic and other forms separately from the functions they can perform).

WHAT MODES ARE THERE?

A starting point from a linguistic perspective might simply differentiate speech from writing. Straight away, though, we will probably notice that things other than words are involved in communication and so we will identify nonverbal communication and notice that this can involve sounds or visuals. This means that we will identify a minimum of four modes: visual nonverbal, visual verbal, aural nonverbal, and aural verbal. In fact, most theorists will identify a wider range and some will point out that it is not easy to differentiate all of the modes involved in any act of communication. Therefore, talking about modes involves a kind of simplification for the purposes of analysis by treating things as more clearly distinct than they probably are.

As you read this chapter, you are probably either looking at ink on a page or light on a screen. So there is a visual mode but a different one in each case. You are also reading so there is a written mode. We might also consider things like the shape of the font, the layout on the page and screen, and so on. If you talk to a friend about the book, many more things will be relevant, including prosody, nonverbal communicative behaviours, things which are not communicative (e.g. you might have a slightly creaky voice following a cold), and some things which are arguably communicative to some extent, e.g. the clothes you are wearing. When I have discussed questions about multimodal communication in class, students have always concluded that all communication is multimodal.

So things are quite complicated. Perhaps paradoxically, part of the job of analysis is to simplify things and treat them as simpler than they are. Still, taking account of these things even in a simplified way means that our accounts of communication are more realistic than accounts which focus only on words.

So what modes might we identify? Bezemer and Jewitt (2018) suggest a useful starting point:

> If a 'means for making meaning' is a 'modality', or 'mode', as it is usually called, then we might say that the term 'multimodality' is a recognition of the fact that people use multiple means of meaning making.
>
> *(Bezemer and Jewitt 2018: 282)*

As mentioned above, much of the research on this has been from the perspective of 'social semiotics', an approach which focuses on how meanings are made and the 'resources' used to make them. Accounts in pragmatics will vary depending on how they view 'meaning making' and the roles of semantics and pragmatics in contributing to that.

A key aim of work on multimodal communication in general is to develop an 'integrated' account, i.e. one which takes account of all of the different kinds of 'modes' and 'semiotic resources' which are involved in communication and how they interact with each other in communicative acts. This fits with a general trend in pragmatics to move away from simplified accounts which focus on only one or a small number of things and to take account more fully of everything which is involved in producing and responding to communicative acts.

To take just one simple example, the way we understand utterances of just the word *yeh* or *yes* (which is far less common in English) is affected by prosody, facial expressions, and bodily movements. If I make a statement and you respond by producing just the word *yeh* with a fairly high pitch range, a rise-fall pitch movement, eyebrows raised, and a nodding head, I am likely to think that you agree with me. If your utterance represents the same word but you do it with a fairly low and quite level pitch, your head pointing downwards, and no nodding head, I am likely to assume that you don't agree with me. To take another example, the way we give directions interacts with whether we point in particular directions, or sometimes move our whole body, while doing so. In text messages, we often add capitalisation, punctuation, and images such as emojis to help our addressees work out what we intend. And so on.

Influential early work by Barthes (1964, 1968) focused on how texts and images interact and how they can constrain interpretations of each other. Barthes used the term 'anchor' for cases where words constrain how we understand images. Advertisements and political campaign posters are useful examples for this. Consider this utterance, for example:

(5) More taxes, more borrowing, more debt.

You can make some assumptions about what it communicates but there are questions you can't answer without access to more contextual assumptions. These words appeared in a political campaign poster from the UK Conservative Party during an election campaign in 2015. You'll guess now that they will be intending to communicate that somebody or something else would lead to more taxes, borrowing, and debt. You can see the text with an accompanying image here:

https://www.itv.com/news/update/2015-04-18/new-tory-poster-shows-sturgeon-as-miliband-puppeteer/

If you know that the person on the left of the image is Nicola Sturgeon, the First Minister of Scotland at the time, and the person on the right is Ed Milliband, then leader of the UK Labour Party, then you'll be able to see that the poster aims to suggest that these things will follow if the Labour Party are elected.

The image shows Milliband as a puppet and Sturgeon controlling him. If you saw this image on its own, you would be likely to follow certain kinds of interpretations, building on general assumptions about the metaphorical idea that the actions of individuals are sometimes controlled by others in ways which can be seen as resembling how a puppet is controlled by a puppeteer. The words below the image encourage us to go down more specific paths in considering what the image conveys. In Barthes's terms, the image and the words 'anchor' each other by leading to more specific interpretations.

We can also, of course, say that the image constrains interpretation of the words.

This kind of metaphorical thinking is quite common and images like this have often been used in political communication. You can find another example here:

https://whip.org.uk/2020/03/27/dominic-cummings-to-lengthen-puppet-strings-to-two-metres-to-enforce-social-distancing/

This image was produced and used by a website speculating on what the UK government would do next during the Covid-19 pandemic and just after Boris Johnson, the UK Prime Minister at the time, pictured on the right, had tested positive for Covid-19. The person on the left is Dominic Cummings, a government adviser often judged to have considerable influence over Johnson and the government. Again, the words above and below this image encourage us to go down more specific paths in considering what the image conveys.

In other cases, we need both the text and the image to understand an overall meaning, e.g. your passport identifies you through the interaction of your photograph and what is written there. Barthes calls this 'relay'.

Forceville (1996, 2005, 2014; see also Yus 2008, 2009) has focused on how we understand comics and graphic novels, looking at how different kinds of cues in the text affect how we understand them, sometimes without being explicitly aware of the formal cues and how they work. One example is the amount of space between 'frames' or 'boxes' in a comic strip or graphic novel. When we look at a page, we 'know' that a smaller gap between two boxes suggests that we move in that direction first rather than moving 'across' a bigger gap.

Comics and graphic novels also often use items which are termed 'runes' (not the same as the marks used in the writing system of Old English). These are small marks such as little lines which indicate motion, speed, and sometimes emotions. It is easy to see how these are related to emoticons and emojis, which are another case where there is some coded meaning.

Like linguistic expressions, emoticons are understood not just by decoding but also by inference. If we say, for example, that this sign:

:-(

'means' sadness, we do not stop there when we see it. If I send this in response to a message from you reporting some bad news, then you will understand that I am saying that I am sad to hear your news and maybe more than that. Notice that these do indicate a bit more as the 'sadness' emoticon would not be appropriate in response to really devastating news where we would be more likely to send a message with words of condolence.

Emojis have been much discussed in media recently, often focusing on the question of whether emojis constitute a 'language'. The answer is clearly no, as emojis are not 'morphemes' and they do not combine as forms in languages do. They can be combined but the way they work together is different from how linguistic expressions function together. However, they do constitute a 'semiotic resource' and they do have encoded meanings. Some theorists, including Kress and van Leeuwen, suggest that visual communication systems have a 'grammar' but this is different from the systems referred to by most linguists when they use the term; similarly, while Barthes and other semioticians use the word 'code' when discussing visual images, they are using it more broadly than it is used in work on linguistic semantics and pragmatics, i.e. to cases where there is no clearly identifiable correspondence between a form and one or more specific meanings.

Some of the encoded meanings in visual communication are clearer and narrower than others, e.g. brand logos are quite specific while emoticons are looser. As with language, emoticons, and nonverbal communication, understanding communication which uses these forms always involves inference, i.e. pragmatic processes.

One question which has been explored recently is the question of whether visual communication can ever be said to be explicit. This has been discussed by Forceville (2011; Forceville et al 2014), partly focusing on examples where visual images seem to have a coded meaning. Forceville and Clark (2014) suggest that we can think of visual communication as having explicit meaning to the extent that there are coded meanings (which are then developed to recover explicit meanings, termed 'explicatures' in relevance theory). On this view, understanding a comic strip involves a combination of decoding of linguistic and other stimuli, recognition of what is represented by 'iconic' representations, and inference of explicatures and implicatures.

We started this section with the observation that work on multimodality aims to move away from approaches which focus mainly or only on linguistic communication and to develop a fuller and 'integrated' account of how we produce and understand communicative acts. It is clear that we are making progress along these lines and that fuller accounts are now available.

PUTTING IT ALL TOGETHER

So far, then, we have seen that work is developing which looks not only at the meanings of linguistic expressions and how they are understood in contexts but also at the effects of prosody, nonverbal, and multimodal communication. Prosody and nonverbal behaviour can have very important effects on how we understand each other. An utterance of just the word *yeh* will be taken very differently depending on its prosodic form, facial expression, and whether the speaker nods their head or not. To explain a particular communicative act, then, we need to identify coded meanings of verbal and nonverbal forms and to account for how they interact in leading to an overall interpretation. We will then have a complex analysis reflecting the complexity of communicative interaction.

FINDING OUT MORE

Here are some ideas for things you might do to develop understanding of ideas in the chapter and to find out more, followed by some suggested further reading.

YOUR OWN EXAMPLES

In looking for and making notes of examples here, you might focus on how understanding is affected by nonverbal behaviour and the inter-action of meanings from different modes.

ADAPTING EXAMPLES

Again, you can find out more by adapting the examples you look at, i.e. by suggesting different formulations. Now that we have looked at more things beyond linguistic forms, you might extend what I suggested at the end of the previous chapter, i.e. altering examples in a wider range of ways. You might imagine keeping prosody, nonverbal, and visual aspects (more or less) the same but changing the words used in an utter-ance. Or change just the prosody, just the nonverbal behaviour, or just the accompanying visuals. Some of what you find is likely to be fairly unsurprising but you might find things that you didn't expect.

FURTHER READING

Again, the ideas discussed in this chapter are not discussed in all pragmatics textbooks (again, I think they should be). Wharton (2009), mentioned at the end of the previous chapter, is a good place to start for pragmatics and nonverbal communication. Here are some sources on multimodal communication:

1. Bezemer, Jeff and Carey Jewitt. 2018. Multimodality: A guide for linguists. In Lia Litosseliti (ed.) *Research Methods in Linguistics*, 2nd edition. Bloomsbury: 281–304.
2. Jewitt, Carey, Jeff Bezemer and Kay O'Halloran. 2016. *Introducing Multimodality*. Routledge.
3. Kress, Gunther and Theo van Leeuwen. 2010. *Multimodality: A Social Semiotic Approach to Contemporary Communication*. Routledge.
4. Machin, David. 2007. *Introduction to Multimodal Analysis*. Hodder Arnold.

THE FUTURE

DEVELOPING PRAGMATIC THEORIES

This final chapter presents some thoughts on what the future might hold for work in pragmatics of the types considered here. It starts with thoughts on where pragmatics has gone since Grice made his influential proposals towards the end of the twentieth century. It then considers some possible future directions and concludes with suggestions for projects which you or other researchers might work on.

WHERE PRAGMATICS HAS GONE

There is no doubt that there have been very significant developments in pragmatics since Grice developed his initial ideas. This section briefly considers some of the most significant developments which followed from Grice's work. Naturally, I have been selective and others would come up with a different list.

PRAGMATICS IS POSSIBLE

To some extent, we could say that Grice's most significant contribution was to show that an account of pragmatic processes is even possible. Many influential thinkers, including some linguists, philosophers, and psychologists continue to doubt this, despite the progress that has been made in understanding pragmatic processes and the many ways in which these ideas have been applied. Arguing from the perspective of relevance theory, Scott-Phillips (2015) suggests that pragmatics is central to understanding language and its evolution. He argues that linguistic systems help to make communication more efficient and that the evolution of linguistic systems follows from the development of the kind of communication which pragmatic theories aim to explain. Seen in this way, pragmatics is absolutely central to understanding communication and linguistics is part of that. This is an inversion of a common view which sees pragmatics as part of linguistics, sometimes as marginal, and sometimes as separate from linguistics. Scott-Phillips's view may not be generally accepted but it is clear that pragmatics is an important area and that theoretical approaches continue to develop.

PRAGMATIC PRINCIPLES

Grice's central idea shares properties with other developments in scientific studies in that it involved postulating something new which interacts with things we already assumed to lead to new explanations (Newton's postulation of the force of gravity is a classic example). We knew about linguistic meanings, we knew that contexts affect meanings, and we knew that the same words said on different occasions can lead to different interpretations. What Grice added was the idea that there are principles which guide interpretations. Current pragmatic theories all assume pragmatic principles different from those proposed by Grice. Some, such as those of Horn and Levinson, are similar but not identical to Gricean maxims. Others, such as the principles in relevance theory, are seen instead as law-like generalisations about human cognition and communication.

As mentioned above, Grice's proposals made assumptions about what speakers as well as hearers do, but the focus following this has been mainly on hearers and it's fair to say that Grice's approach was largely hearer-focused. His key notions and distinctions mainly focus on interpretation, with the overarching idea being that pragmatic principles are involved in cases of non-natural meaning and in deriving implicatures.

Pragmatics since then has developed a number of important new ideas building on Grice's initial suggestions. Some of these fill in gaps which Grice was aware of and discussed. Some built on problems identified with Grice's approach by other theorists. Some have arisen from new understanding of the processes involved in communication (in production, interpretation, and evaluation). As mentioned above, the list of things considered here is not exhaustive. It's also not arranged chronologically.

RATIONALITY

Grice assumed that rational principles guide hearers (and readers and viewers) in arriving at interpretations. Some later theorists have followed Grice in assuming this. Horn's and Levinson's approaches, for example, can be seen as proposing principles which can be applied in order to make rational inferences about what is communicated. Not all later theorists have stuck so closely to this view. Relevance theory can be seen as retaining the idea that pragmatic principles are ultimately rational but they view comprehension as involving a heuristic which operates quickly and without the kind of explicit reasoning assumed by Grice. Allott (2013) suggests that the kind of rationality assumed by relevance theory is an evolutionary, adaptive one, i.e. that cognitive systems have developed in such ways that their processes can be understood as ultimately rational. The processes do not, though, involve the kinds of explicit, conscious inference which we associate with reasoning of the type assumed by Grice. Mercier and Sperber (2017) develop a fuller account of the nature of pragmatic inference, viewing it as emerging for the purposes of argumentation (from the perspectives of communicators, who want to be trusted and believed, and of addressees, who do not want to be misled). They also differentiate spontaneous pragmatic inference from more explicit, conscious reasoning. Other theorists, e.g. Recanati (1993, 2003) distinguish 'primary pragmatic processes', involved in such things as disambiguation and reference assignment, seeing these as 'associative' rather than inferential.

COMMUNICATION AS INTERACTION

As we saw in Chapters 3 to 5, another development has been increased attention to the role of communicators and the interaction of communicators in constructing meanings. Rather than focusing mainly on how addressees respond to individual utterances, there has been increased focus on what communicators do in producing utterances and on how interacting communicators construct meanings together. Alongside this, there has been increased interest in how communicated meanings emerge during whole interactions and on how meanings can be constructed before and after, as well as during, interactive behaviour.

PRAGMATICS AND WHAT IS SAID

As we have seen, a key development has been the recognition that pragmatic processes are involved in working out what is explicitly communicated ('what is said' for Grice) as well as what is indirectly communicated (implicatures). Pragmaticists have also recognised that there is more to working out explicitly communicated meanings than Grice had envisaged and we now have a much fuller understanding of what is involved in inferring explicit meanings than previously (as well, of course, as debates around the details of all of this).

NONVERBAL COMMUNICATION

While Grice termed his ideas a 'theory of conversation', he made clear that he was not claiming to have developed a full theory but rather to suggest the direction in which such a theory might develop. The term 'conversation' is also misleading as it suggests a focus only on spoken interactions. Grice's first lecture and paper included an example of written communication in the form of a letter of reference for a job as a philosophy lecturer. Clearly, then, Grice's ideas are relevant to written as well as spoken communication.

As we've seen, it's also clear that pragmatic principles also apply to nonverbal communication. If I ask how you are and you respond by picking up a bottle of aspirins and holding it in front of me, you clearly intend me to infer something from this and pragmatic principles will guide the interpretation process.

THE NATURE OF IMPLICATURES

There has been considerable work on the nature of implicatures and of course there are different views about them. Some theorists (e.g. Horn and Levinson) have continued to assume a distinction between something like what Grice termed 'generalised' and 'particularised' conversational implicatures, even if the terms they use are different. Others (e.g. Sperber and Wilson) have rejected this distinction, assuming that all implicatures are derived in the same way and governed by pragmatic principles. Some theories also assume that implicatures are more or less strongly communicated rather than being simply communicated or not. By contrast, very few if any theorists now recognise Grice's category of 'conventional implicature', reanalysing these phenomena as particular kinds of linguistic meaning.

THE NATURE OF MEANING

Grice's ideas about meaning, about different kinds of 'meaning' and about the kinds of meanings relevant to verbal communication, have been hugely influential and also much debated since. While, again, there is no consensus on this, it is clear that this is a difficult issue and that identifying particular varieties of meaning is not an easy task. One significant idea, developed by Sperber and Wilson (1986, 1995; Wharton 2009) is that there is not as sharp a distinction as Grice assumed between cases of what he called 'non-natural meaning' and other types.

MULTIMODAL MEANINGS

As well as considering nonverbal communication, a significant amount of work has now been carried out on multimodal communication. The role of pragmatics in understanding how all of the various aspects of multimodal texts (which some would say means all texts) is not always discussed explicitly in these analyses but it is clear that pragmatic principles play a role and some accounts focus on the pragmatic processes involved in multimodal meaning.

MOVING AWAY FROM SENTENCES AND PROPOSITIONS

Several of the above points could be related to the more general idea that work on semantics and pragmatics no longer focuses mainly on sentences and propositions. Traditionally, work on logic and philosophy assumed that sentences are key units in language and that propositions are what they usually convey. Work in pragmatics has shown that not all utterances contain expressions with representational meanings, that sentences do not have fixed linguistic meanings, that the meanings of sentences are not necessarily propositions, and that utterances do not always or only give rise to propositional meanings.

PRAGMATICS AND THE MIND

Much of the work discussed in this book considers pragmatics with a focus on the mind and cognitive processes. There has been considerable development over the years in thinking about the nature of the mind and the cognitive structures and processes involved in pragmatics. A range of views exist on this now, including approaches which view language as distinct from other aspects of cognition and those that do not see a principled distinction. Some discussion has focused on technical details, considering, for example, whether pragmatic processes involve one or more dedicated mental 'modules', i.e. components of the mind with a specific domain and their own specific kinds of processes. Sometimes, discussion focuses on what kinds of modules are involved if so. This is markedly different from Grice's approach, which did not make any explicit commitments with regard to how his ideas related to the mind.

PRAGMATICS AND SOCIAL INTERACTION

While the approaches discussed in this book vary with regard to how much they focus on social structures and phenomena, they all say more about social phenomena than Grice did. There is a greater focus on all of the features which interact in social exchanges and consideration of how cognitive and social aspects interact. Mercier and Sperber (2017), for example, argue that intentional communication and the pragmatic principles which govern interaction arose for social reasons. Grice's approach did not make any explicit claims about pragmatic principles understood as social or cognitive phenomena.

(IM)POLITENESS

As we have seen, a major growth area in pragmatics has been work on politeness and impoliteness. We know far more now about the details of the 'facework' involved in interaction. This relates to the previous point, as facework is very much about how we manage our social standing and our social relationships.

PRAGMATIC STYLISTICS

Another growth area has been in work which focuses on how texts are produced, interpreted, and evaluated, i.e. on stylistics (for discussion, see Chapman and Clark 2014, 2019; Locher and Jucker 2017, 2021). This work constitutes one of the most important applications and tests of ideas from pragmatics. While there was immediate interest in how Grice's ideas could be applied in this area, there has been significantly more work on this in recent years and a wider range of approaches have been applied.

CLINICAL APPLICATIONS

Pragmatics has been applied in a range of clinical contexts (for discussion, see Cummings 2009, 2017). This has been another growth area with ideas from pragmatics contributing more both in understanding the nature of particular clinical conditions and in contributing to ways of diagnosing them. This has included work on conditions such as the autism spectrum, various kinds of dementia, and aspects of typical and atypical development.

TESTING PRAGMATIC THEORIES

A very important development which there has not been space to discuss here is in the far wider range of methods now used to test ideas from pragmatic theories. Grice's ideas were developed mainly based on intuitions about utterances and logical and conceptual discussion. This continued in much of the work which followed from and built on Grice's ideas. In the 1990s, dissatisfaction with this limited range of approaches led to the development of experimental and other methods. Experimental pragmatics is now a large and growing field (for discussion, see Noveck 2018; Noveck and Sperber 2004) and pragmaticists now also rely on observational and corpus data (Aijmer and Rühlemann 2015; Rühlemann 2019). Work in stylistics and in clinical applications can also be seen as ways of testing theoretical ideas.

WHERE PRAGMATICS MIGHT GO

There are many unanswered (or only partially answered) questions about pragmatics which pragmatic theorists might focus on in future and it's hard to predict what exactly they will be. It's important for any discipline to be open both to new research directions and to contributions from new researchers so this book finishes by running through some possible future directions and including ideas for projects that some of you might be interested in developing.

Before Grice's ideas were shared, no-one could have predicted how pragmatic theories would develop and expand their scope. It's also impossible to know what will happen next. But I hope these suggestions encourage some of you to find out more and think about contributing to the next range of developments. Most of these suggestions relate to topics I have already discussed.

PRAGMATIC PRINCIPLES AND PROCESSING

Of course, central questions in pragmatics are about exactly what principles guide communication and the details of the processes involved. These are key but very difficult questions. Following Grice's initial work, theorists have moved in different directions in developing claims about both the principles governing pragmatic processes and the processes themselves. Neo-Griceans view pragmatic principles as similar to the maxims proposed by Grice while relevance theorists view them as generalisations about human cognition and communication. Levinson has proposed heuristics associated with the principles while relevance theorists have proposed a 'fast and frugal' heuristic which guides interpretation. These approaches suggest differences in exactly how pragmatic inference takes place, e.g. in how much explicit reasoning is involved and in how particular processes are likely to go. For Grice, all pragmatic reasoning should be calculable so that we could spell out the reasoning behind the derivation of all implicatures. This is not assumed to be true for all pragmatic inferencing in more recent approaches. As well as the assumption that there are heuristics, which allows room for variation and error, some pragmatic processes are also assumed to be 'associative', which means they are quite different from the kind of logical reasoning assumed by Grice. Future work will surely explore these different assumptions more closely and test and develop them. This might involve looking for evidence about the extent to which individuals can be aware of the nature of pragmatic processes and principles, the extent to which they resemble or differ from other kinds of processes involved in reasoning, and how they can be affected by different kinds of cognitive and social phenomena. It might also consider the extent to which pragmatic processes interact with other cognitive processes and how, which relates to more general questions about pragmatics and the mind.

PRODUCTION AND INTERACTION

As mentioned above, there has been increased interest recently in the pragmatic processes involved in producing communicative acts and the relationships between the inferences of communicators and addressees. Future work is likely to focus on developing fuller accounts of this and so to develop fuller accounts of how individuals interact to affect what is communicated, and on how this extends over whole interactions and beyond (i.e. on what happens before and after people are communicating with each other).

IDENTITY

There has also been increased interest recently in how identities are constructed by communicative behaviour. This includes how individuals aim to perform their own identities, how they attribute identities to others, and how interactive behaviour affects identity construction. Work on (im)politeness and facework is relevant here and focusing on identity construction can help us to understand how behaviour can give rise to and enhance or reduce conflicts and senses of group solidarity.

PRAGMATICS AND WHAT IS SAID

As we have seen, there has been considerable focus over the years on how pragmatic processes are involved in working out what is explicitly communicated ('what is said' for Grice) as well as what is indirectly communicated (implicatures). Future projects might focus on resolving ongoing debates such as the one about whether all of the things inferred in understanding what is explicitly communicated originate in linguistically encoded meanings and on the nature of enrichment processes.

PROSODY, NONVERBAL, AND MULTIMODAL COMMUNICATION

Future work will surely develop fuller understanding of the nature of prosodic meaning, of nonverbal communication, on the contribution of particular nonverbal behaviours, and on how various kinds of behaviours interact. We have much fuller understanding now of how multimodal texts are produced and understood. Future work will surely develop this further and lead to fuller accounts of the complexities of the production and understanding of multimodal texts.

THE NATURE OF IMPLICATURES

An ongoing debate has been on the nature of implicatures, particularly whether we can distinguish a kind of 'default' category similar to Grice's notion of generalised conversational implicature from those which only arise on the basis of specific aspects of particular contexts. Future research is likely to focus on this, on the ways in which individuals vary with regard to which inferences they make, and what contributes to that.

MOVING AWAY FROM SENTENCES AND PROPOSITIONS

A key change in work since Grice has been an ongoing move away from the assumptions that sentences are key units in language and that what is communicated can be understood as sets of propositions. Grice himself, of course, distinguished sentence meanings from speaker meanings (or utterance meanings) and showed that speaker meanings are the most important ones in verbal interactions. More recent work has moved much further than this small step by Grice. There has also been consideration of what are termed 'non-propositional' meanings or effects. This includes emotional and affective responses as well as the idea that some communicative acts give rise to visual images. Figurative language (metaphor, irony, etc.) is often associated with emotional and non-propositional effects and so this work connects closely with ongoing work on figurative language.

PRAGMATIC STYLISTICS

This has been another significant growth area, particularly in the twenty-first century. We are continuing to find out more about the roles pragmatic processes play in the production, interpretation, and evaluation of texts. As with pragmatics in general, there has been a tendency to focus mainly on how texts are understood. There is likely to be more work in future on the processes involved in producing and evaluating texts.

CLINICAL APPLICATIONS

Work on clinical pragmatics has also increased over the years, with ideas from pragmatics applied and tested in accounting for, understanding, and diagnosing a range of clinical conditions. There will surely be far more work on this in coming years.

THE SEMANTICS-PRAGMATICS DISTINCTION

There have been debates about how to draw the semantics-pragmatics distinction since as long as there has been recognition of pragmatics. There are many different proposals about how to draw the distinction, as well as how to distinguish linguistic from non-linguistic phenomena in the mind and in society. Grice seemed to see implicature as the main thing which pragmatics was about (although he never used the term 'pragmatics' in the sense used in this book). More recently, pragmatics has been seen to play a role in explicit as well as implicit communication. Some approaches draw a sharp distinction between semantics and pragmatics, often seeing semantics as being to do with linguistically encoded meanings. Others take a looser view. Ideas about the nature of sentences and propositions are also relevant here, with some theorists seeing semantics as being about idealised sentences or propositions and therefore distinct from the processes involved in communicative interaction. Again, there is still much to debate here.

LINGUISTIC SEMANTICS AND LANGUAGE VARIATION AND CHANGE

Semantics and pragmatics depend on each other. We cannot propose semantic analyses without considering how they contribute to interpretations in specific contexts and we cannot account for interpretations in contexts without considering the contribution of linguistic meanings (unless we take the philosophical or idealised view mentioned just above here). There is much work to do on understanding what linguistic forms contribute, how they are understood in contexts, and how pragmatic processes are involved in changes in meaning. As mentioned, changes in use of the word *basic*, which appears in the title of this book, could form the 'basis' for a case study.

FINDING OUT MORE

Here are some ideas for projects you might work on (so a bit more than the kinds of exercises suggested at the end of other chapters) to develop understanding of ideas in the chapter and to find out more, followed by some suggested further reading.

SOME POSSIBLE PROJECTS

Of course, the boundary between exercises to develop understanding and research projects is not a clear one. They both involve doing things in order to find out more. These are just some ways I've thought of for you to start exploring some topics in pragmatics. There are, of course, many more.

One way of exploring topics is to read some of the literature on them, critically considering the arguments developed there and the kinds of evidence used for different views. Some arguments in pragmatics are conceptual or logical, i.e. they involve thinking through what has been claimed to see whether the steps in the arguments make sense and how sure we can be that the conclusions follow from the starting assumptions. It is hard to gather clear empirical evidence on all of these but some work has been done, and another way forward is to consider existing evidence and how it has been interpreted. In pragmatics, it's always useful to look at examples so it's a good idea to focus on noticing interesting uses of language and to take a note of them when you do. An example you find interesting today could play an important role in a project in the future.

ETHICS AND SAFETY

Remember that there are ethical issues if you work with human participants on any of these projects. You shouldn't start working with participants before thinking these through and putting your plans through an ethical approval process if possible.

It's important to recognise that we don't always recognise ethical issues in advance and sometimes ethical issues arise only after we begin working on a project so it's a good idea to find out more and get some advice before working on a project. Some places where you can find out more include the British Association for Applied Linguistics Good Practice Guide (https://www.baal.org.uk/wp-con tent/uploads/2021/03/BAAL-Good-Practice-Guidelines-2021.pdf; there's also a shorter version of this for students at: https://www.baa l.org.uk/wp-content/uploads/2017/08/goodpractice_stud.pdf),   the Singapore Statement on Research Integrity (https://wcrif.org/do cuments/327-singapore-statement-a4size), and the Association of Internet Researchers ethics page (https://aoir.org/ethics/). There's also useful advice in textbooks, e.g. a chapter in Wray and Bloomer (2012: 184–188), one by Penelope Eckert in the collection edited by Podesva and Sharma (2014: 11–26), and one by Christine Mallinson in the collection edited by Lia Litosseliti (2018: 57–84).

It's also important to think through risks associated with particular kinds of investigations and to go through a risk assessment process. Students and researchers sometimes come up with ideas which could put themselves at risk of mental or physical harm, e.g. approaching strangers in the street, interviewing participants in their own homes or offices. Researchers always need to think through the risks involved and how to design projects to minimise them.

PRAGMATIC PRINCIPLES AND PROCESSING

a. *Explicit reasoning and intuitive interpretations*

Consider how you might arrive at a particular interpretation using explicit reasoning. You might do this following the process suggested by Grice or in some other way. Consider to what extent it is possible to arrive at the interpretation by explicit reasoning. Are there cases where this does not seem possible?

b. *Comparing interpretations*

Compare the interpretations different people give of the same commu-nicative act. You might do this informally just by noticing when people understand things differently (e.g. where one person thinks somebody has been rude but another person disagrees) or you might create situations where you record interpretations, e.g. by presenting people with spoken, written, or video-recorded communicative acts and asking them to indicate how they understood them. Consider how they vary and what could be possible explanations for the differences. If pragmatic principles are common to all of the people involved, as many pragmatic theorists believe, then there must be another explanation, e.g. varying access to contextual assumptions. You might include here cases where the same person understands something differently in one situation rather than another, e.g. responding differently to a comment from a friend when it's late and you're tired as opposed to when you have more energy, or responding more or less positively to an artwork the second time you engage with it. People often report a different evaluation of a book, film, play, or other kind of artwork when they encounter it a second time.

PRODUCTION AND INTERACTION

a. *What speakers and writers do*

Look at particular interactions and notice cases where there is evidence about something affecting what communicators say or do. This could, for example, include hesitations or reformulations. Look out, also, for features which seem to have something to do with (im)politeness or the construction of identity.

b. *Comparing communication*

It can be useful to notice how people speak or write differently in different situations, e.g. how we begin an email message to a friend as opposed to a work colleague. You might also create tasks to generate comparisons, e.g. ask your participants to indicate what they would say or write, varying who they are addressing each time. Remember here to pay attention also to nonverbal behaviour which can give interesting clues about what communicators are doing.

PRAGMATICS AND WHAT IS SAID

a. *Kinds of enrichment*

As we've seen, there is debate about what kinds of processes are involved in arriving at 'directly communicated' meanings ('what is said') and whether there are always linguistic cues which lead to the various kinds of enrichment. Look at example utterances, identify what you think has been, or is likely to be, added to linguistic meanings in arriving at 'what is said'. Can they be explained without assuming pragmatic inference is involved? You might follow this up by asking others how they have understood particular utterances (remember, though, that we can't assume that what people say they have done always reflects what they actually have done).

b. *Lexical meanings*

One topic not much discussed in this book is the idea that we adjust the meanings of individual words when we understand utterances. If I ask if anyone can see a *pen* when I'm using a whiteboard in class, students will probably look for a whiteboard marker. If I ask for one when sitting at a desk in a meeting, my colleagues will probably assume I want something like a biro for taking notes on paper. There are also more creative uses, and some approaches to non-literal language and metaphor assume that this involves changing understanding of lexical items, e.g. when I say that my best friend is a *lifesaver* when they offer me a biscuit, I don't mean that they have prevented from dying around that time but I do mean that I am very grateful. You could begin a project by gathering examples of these adjusted meanings and considering how they are likely to be understood. Again, you could also ask others to discuss how they understand them. You might also look at examples where a word is used with adjusted meanings during one piece of artistic work, e.g. a song or a novel. I have been gathering examples of uses of the word *2020* at the moment, e.g. I noticed a headline the other day which said 'when 2020 dishes up another helping of 2020'. Working on this project might lead you into research on metaphor and figurative language more generally.

NONVERBAL AND MULTIMODAL COMMUNICATION

a. *Gathering examples*

There is lots of scope here to investigate particular behaviours and what they mean. You could begin by looking at examples of verbal communication and noticing what people do with their bodies other than producing spoken or signed expressions. Begin by categorising them as beat gestures, emblems, pantomimes, or something else, and then look at the details of what they do. It's interesting to consider to what extent particular meanings have become encoded or conventional and to what extent they rely on pragmatic inference.

b. *Multimodal texts*

Of course, most and arguably all communicative acts are multimodal. As a subpart of your project, or a separate one, you might examine particular multimodal texts which are written or recorded and look at all of the elements within them to consider how they work together to create meanings. Again, it is interesting to look at specific elements in detail and consider to what extent the communicator is using an established convention and to what extent they are being innovative and/or creative.

EXPLORING IMPLICATURES

a. *Specific examples*

Look at a collection of examples of spoken or written texts, identify implicatures they are likely to give rise to and consider how to explain how they are arrived at with reference to the approaches discussed in this book.

b. *Comparing and revising texts*

If you know of examples of texts which exist in more than one version, you can compare them with regard to the implicatures they are likely to generate. Many literary works, including songs, plays, and films, exist in more than one version. Sometimes performances of scripts differ from what was originally written. It's interesting to explore the effects of different versions. It's also interesting (and fun) to come up with your own revisions of texts. A striking example is the book *Gender Swapped Fairy Tales* by Karrie Fransman and Jonathan Plackett (Faber & Faber, 2020) which contains a collection of fairy tales where a computer programme simply went through each text and swapped the gender of any term associated with a gender, so that *he* became *she, man* became *woman, Beauty and the Beast* became *Handsome and the Beast*, and so on. It's fascinating to look at the effects of these changes.

NON-PROPOSITIONAL MEANINGS

a. *Non-propositional effects in interpretation*

Gather any examples you notice where a text seems to have a meaning which is not propositional, e.g. when it generates excitement or sadness, or when it makes you think of one or more images. Make a note of the non-propositional effect and consider how it arises. To what extent can this be explained in terms of pragmatic inference?

b. *Non-propositional production*

Gather any examples you notice where the way somebody communicates seems to be affected by things which are not propositional such as emotions or tiredness. How do you think these affect production? Do you think they give rise to meanings? If so, are these intentional or not? What is the difference between somebody intentionally and unintentionally giving rise to such interpretations?

LINGUISTIC SEMANTICS AND LANGUAGE VARIATION AND CHANGE

a. *Linguistic meanings*

Choose a particular linguistic expression and consider what it contributes to meanings in particular contexts. What must its linguistically encoded meaning be? This might seem to be a question about semantics rather than pragmatics but notice that you need to consider how the expressions are understood in contexts in order to make assumptions about their linguistic meanings.

b. *Variation and change*

Consider forms which are used differently by different people or groups, e.g. the word *canny* is used differently by many speakers in Newcastle from how it used by speakers of other varieties of English;

one piece of evidence for this is that speakers in Newcastle use it before the word *good* as in '*that's canny good*' which does not appear in the speech of most speakers of other varieties. Consider what the differences are and how they lead to different kinds of interpretations. Note that some of these will contribute to ideas about identity.

You can also consider here expressions whose meanings have changed over time (remembering that accounting for variation in meaning always involves an account of how meanings have changed over time). Consider meanings which have changed recently or in the more distant past. What role could pragmatics play in explaining this? To take one example, in time-telling contexts, *half two* for some speakers used to mean the same as *half past one* where it now usually means *half past two*. Can we explain this by considering how younger people might have understood utterances containing this phrase (often before they have learned how to tell the time from a clock or watch)?

GLOSSARY

This glossary contains a list of key terms which have been used in work on pragmatics. As with any research area, there are key technical terms which pragmaticists use, and it helps to be aware of these and to develop some understanding of them early. As also often happens, there is disagreement about some of the terms. It is important to be aware of the nature of the disagreements. Some are relatively minor, amounting mainly to questions of labelling, e.g. where one term is used to refer to different things by different theorists. More significant disagreements affect the nature of understanding and theory. For example, there is a significant difference between the understanding of the term *ambiguity* to refer to a linguistic expression with more than one encoded meaning and more general difficulties in understanding utterances in contexts. I have kept these brief and not discussed difficult issues and disagreements about terms here.

Ambiguity In linguistics, ambiguity usually refers to linguistic expressions with more than one ('linguistically encoded') meaning, such as *scale*, which can refer (among other things) to part of what covers a fish or to a series of musical notes. Linguists also distinguish **lexical ambiguity**, where a word has more than one meaning (such as *scale*) from **structural** or **syntactic ambiguity**, where a word has more than one category (e.g. *scale* can also be a verb meaning to climb something or to remove scales from a fish, among other things) or a sequence of words can be associated with more than one structure, e.g. a *big data research textbook* could refer to a data research textbook which is big or to a research textbook on big data (there are other possibilities too!)

Concept A mental representation of something in the world.

Context Most generally, contexts are things which affect what other things means. For an everyday spoken utterance, contexts are things other than linguistic meanings which affect how we understand them. We can also think about the contexts for nonverbal and multimodal communication. Contextual assumptions need to be mentally represented in order to affect interpretations. Many theories assume that contexts are dynamic and affected by interactions and interpretation processes. Social and cultural contexts are made up of socially or culturally relevant features of where interactions take place. Logical contexts are logical or propositional forms which affect what can be concluded from other forms. For example, $P \rightarrow Q$ ('*if P then Q*') entails Q in the context of P (i.e. we can conclude Q from '*if P then Q*' if we also know that 'P' is true) and vice versa.

Explicature A technical term in relevance theory for a communicated assumption which is developed from the linguistic meaning of an utterance (the term replaces Grice's 'what is said' and represents a different understanding of what is explicitly communicated).

Implication/imply In general, an implication is something that follows from something else. If I am speaking, it follows (i.e. this **implies**) that I am alive and able to speak. If it rains in a context where we know that my flowers need water, this implies that my flowers will get some water. The term is used loosely and this is a motivation for Grice to coin the more technical term **implicature**.

Implicature A technical term coined by Grice to refer to implications which are intentionally communicated.

Infer A term describing the process of working out conclusions on the basis of other assumptions or communicative behaviour. In everyday communication, the term is often used to refer to what somebody intends to communicate. In linguistic semantics and pragmatics, inference is usually used to refer to how we understand things rather than what we aim to communicate.

Maxims Principles suggested by Grice to account for how we understand utterances in contexts. Grice suggested that communicators aim to follow these and that addressees assume that they are observed overall even if what is said on its own seems not to follow them. Addressees infer implicatures because they assume the maxims must be being followed overall.

Neo-Gricean pragmatics Approaches to pragmatics which build on Grice's work and retain the assumption that there are maxim-like principles which guide communication and understanding.

Post-Gricean pragmatics While, strictly speaking, all pragmatic theories which follow and build on Grice's ideas are post-Gricean, the term is mainly used to refer to approaches (such as relevance theory) which build on Grice's work but do not assume maxim-like principles.

Pragmatics The study of how we produce and understand communicative behaviour. As with many theoretical terms, this can refer to the processes involved in interaction or to the study of, and theories about, them.

Proposition A term used in logic and philosophy as well as linguistics to refer to something which could be evaluated to see whether it is true or false. Strictly speaking, most utterances do not express propositions on their own. We need to make inferences to work out what proposition they represent, e.g. an utterance of the expression *it's on* could express the proposition that the light switch in my living-room at a specific time is in the position which means that power is travelling to the light-bulb or that a specific sports event has been confirmed as going ahead.

Reference/referring expressions Referring expressions are linguistic forms which are to be understood as identifying things or ideas. Part of understanding utterances involves identifying the referents of referring expressions. Referring expressions include words such as *they, she, he, tomorrow, soon, here, now*, phrases such as *the student whose mic isn't working*, and names such as *Billy, Dua Lipa*, or *Newcastle*.

Semantics Linguistic semantics is the study of the encoded meanings of linguistic expressions. A broader sense of semantics refers to the study of meanings more generally. Linguistic semantics often focuses on the link between linguistic expressions and mental representations. A full account of the semantics of linguistic expressions would also need to account for the meanings of mental representations.

Sentence An expression in a language. Since languages are usually thought of as cognitive or abstract phenomena, sentences do not have physical properties. When we say that we have read, written, heard, spoken, or signed a sentence, we are using the term loosely.

Strictly speaking we are referring to utterances which are taken to represent sentences.

Utterance A physical communicative act which involves linguistic communication. Utterances take place in specific times and places and have physical properties. They can, for example, be louder or quieter (sentences cannot). Early work on pragmatics (e.g. Grice's approach) assumed that semantics focused on sentence meaning while pragmatics focused on utterance-meaning (or speaker-meaning).

REFERENCES

Aijmer, Karin and Christoph Rühlemann. (eds.). 2015. *Corpus Pragmatics: A Handbook*. Cambridge University Press.

Alibali, Martha W., Dana C. Heath and Heather J. Myers. 2001. Effects of visibility between speaker and listener on gesture production: some gestures are meant to be seen. *Journal of Memory and Language* 44: 169–188.

Allott, Nicholas. 2013. Relevance theory. In Alessandro Capone, Franco Lo Piparo and Marco Carapezza (eds.) *Perspectives on Pragmatics and Philosophy*, volume 2. Springer: 57–98.

Bach, Kent. 1994. Conversational impliciture. *Mind and Language* 9: 124–162.

Bach, Kent. 1999. The myth of conventional implicature. *Linguistics and Philosophy* 22: 327–366.

Barthes, Roland. 1964. The rhetoric of the image. In Roland Barthes (ed.) *Image-Music-Text*. Fontana: 32–51.

Barthes, Roland. 1968. *Elements of Semiology*. Hill and Wang.

Beckman, Mary E. and Julia Hirschberg. 1994. The ToBI annotation conventions. Online manuscript. http://www.cs.columbia.edu/~julia/files/conv.pdf

Berwick, Robert C. and Noam Chomsky. 2016. *Why Only Us? Language and Evolution*. MIT Press.

Blakemore, Diane. 1987. *Semantic Constraints on Relevance*. Wiley-Blackwell.

Blakemore, Diane. 2002. *Relevance and Linguistic Meaning: The Semantics and Pragmatics of Discourse Markers*. Cambridge University Press, Cambridge.

Brown, Penelope and Stephen C. Levinson. 1987. *Politeness: Some Universals in Language Usage*. Cambridge University Press.

Carston, Robyn and Alison Hall. 2012. Implicature and explicature. In Hans-Jörg Schmid (ed.) *Cognitive Pragmatics*. De Gruyter Mouton: 47–84.

Chapman, Siobhan and Billy Clark (eds.) 2014. *Pragmatic Literary Stylistics*. Palgrave Macmillan.

Chapman, Siobhan and Billy Clark (eds.) 2019. *Pragmatics and Literature*. John Benjamins.

Culpeper, Jonathan. 1996. Towards an anatomy of impoliteness. *Journal of Pragmatics* 25: 349–367.

Cummings, Louise. 2009. *Clinical Pragmatics*. Cambridge University Press.

Cummings, Louise (ed.) 2017. *Research in Clinical Pragmatics*. Springer.

Davidson, Donald. 1967. Truth and meaning. *Synthèse* 17: 304–323. Reprinted in Donald Davidson. 2001. *Inquiries into Truth and Interpretation*. Clarendon Press: 17–42.

Ekman, Paul and Wallace V. Friesen. 1969. The repertoire of non-verbal behaviour categories: origins, usage and coding. *Semiotica* 1: 49–98.

Everett , Daniel. 2005. Cultural constraints on grammar and cognition in Pirahã. *Current Anthropology* 46.4: 621–646.

Everett, Daniel. 2008 *Don't Sleep, There Are Snakes: Life and Language in the Amazonian Jungle*. Profile Books.

Forceville, Charles J. 1996. *Pictorial Metaphor in Advertising*. Routledge.

Forceville, Charles J. 2005. Addressing an audience: time, place, and genre in Peter Van Straaten's calendar cartoons. *Humor* 18: 247–278.

Forceville, Charles J. 2011. Pictorial runes in *Tintin and the Picaros. Journal of Pragmatics* 43(3): 875–890.

Forceville, Charles J. 2014. Relevance theory as model for analysing visual and multimodal communication. In David Machin (ed.) *Visual Communication*. Mouton de Gruyter, 51–70.

Forceville, Charles J. and Billy Clark. 2014. Can pictures have explicatures? *Linguagem em (Dis)curso* 14(3): 1–22 .

Forceville Charles, J., Elizabeth El Refaie and Gert Meesters. 2014. Stylistics and comics. In Michael Burke (ed.) *Routledge Handbook of Stylistics*. Routledge: 485–499.

Goffman, Erving. 1967. *Interaction Ritual: Essays on Face-to-Face Behaviour*. Pantheon Books.

Goffman, Erving. 1981. *Forms of Talk*. University of Pennsylvania Press.

Grice, H. Paul. 1975. Logic and conversation. In Peter Cole and Jerry L. Morgan (eds.) *Syntax and Semantics 3: Speech Acts*. Academic Press: 41–58. Reprinted in Grice 1989: 86–116.

Grice, H. Paul 1978. Further notes on logic and conversation. In Peter Cole (ed.) *Syntax and Semantics, Vol. 9, Pragmatics*. Academic Press: 113–28. Reprinted in Grice 1989: 41–57.

Grice, H. Paul. 1989. *Studies in the Way of Words*. Harvard University Press.

Hauser, Marc. 1996. *The Evolution of Communication*. MIT Press.

Hauser, Marc, Noam Chomsky and W. Tecumseh Fitch. 2002. The faculty of language: what is it, who has it, and how did it evolve? *Science* 298: 1569–1579.

Hockett, Charles F. 1960. The origin of speech. *Scientific American* 203: 88–111.

Hockett, Charles F. 1966. The problem of universals in language. In Joseph Greenberg (ed.) *Universals of Language*. MIT Press: 1–29.

Katz, Jerrold J. and Jerry A. Fodor. 1963. The structure of a semantic theory. *Language* 39: 170–210.

Keenan, Elinor O. 1976. The universality of conversational postulates. *Language in Society* 5.1: 67–80.

Kendon, Adam. 1988. How gestures can become like words? In Fernando Poyatos (ed.) *Cross-Cultural Perspectives in Nonverbal Communication*. Hogrefe: 131–141.

Kendon, Adam. 2004. *Gesture: Visible Action as Utterance*. Cambridge University Press.

Leech Geoffrey N. 1977. *Language and Tact*. Linguistic Agency University of Trier, Series A, Paper No. 46.

Levinson, Stephen C. 1983. *Pragmatics*. Cambridge University Press.

Litosseliti, Lia (ed.) 2018. *Research Methods in Linguistics*, 2nd edition. Bloomsbury.

Locher, Miriam A. and Andreas Jucker (eds.) 2017. *Pragmatics of Fiction*. De Gruyter Mouton.

Locher, Miriam A., and Andreas Jucker. 2021. *The Pragmatics of Fiction: Literature, Stage and Screen Discourse*. Edinburgh University Press

McNeill, David. 1992. *Hand and Mind: What Gestures Reveal About Thought*. University of Chicago Press.

Mercier, Hugo and Dan Sperber. 2017. *The Enigma of Reason: A New Theory of Human Understanding*. Penguin.

Noveck, Ira. 2018. *Experimental Pragmatics*. Cambridge University Press.

Noveck, Ira and Dan Sperber (eds.) 2004. *Experimental Pragmatics*. Palgrave Macmillan.

O'Connor, Joseph D. and Gordon F. Arnold. 1973. *The Intonation of Colloquial English*, 2nd edition. Longman.

Pierrehumbert, Janet and Julia Hirschberg. 1990. The meaning of intonational contours in the interpretation of discourse. In P. Cohen, J. Morgan and M. Pollack (eds.) *Intentions in Communication*. MIT Press: 271–311.

Pitrelli, John F., Mary E. Beckman and Julia Hirschberg. 1994. Evaluation of prosodic transcription labelling reliability in the ToBI framework. *Proceedings of the 1994 International Conference on Spoken Language Processing (PLACE)*: 123–126.

Podesva, Robert J. and Devyani Sharma (eds.) 2014. *Research Methods in Linguistics*. Cambridge University Press.

Recanati, Francois. 1993. *Direct Reference: From Language to Thought*. Wiley-Blackwell.

Recanati, Francois. 2003. *Literal Meaning: The Very Idea*. Cambridge University Press.

Rühlemann, Christoph. 2019. *Corpus Linguistics for Pragmatics*. Routledge.

Scott-Phillips, Thom. 2015. *Speaking Our Minds: Why Human Communication is Different, and How Language Evolved to Make It Special*. Palgrave Macmillan.

Searle, John R. 1975. Indirect speech acts. In Peter Cole and Jerry L. Morgan (eds.) *Syntax and Semantics Volume 3: Speech Acts*. Academic Press: 59–82.

Semino, Elena. 2014. Language, mind and autism in Mark Haddon's the curious incident of the dog in the night-time. In Monika Fludernik and Daniel Jacob (eds.) *Linguistics and Literary Studies*. De Gruyter: 279–303.

Silverman, Kim, Mary E. Beckman, John Pitrelli, Mari Ostendorf, Janet Pierrehumbert, Colin Wightman, Patti Price, and Julia Hirschberg.1992. ToBI: a standard scheme for labelling prosody. International Conference Spoken Language Processing: 867–869.

Sperber, Dan and Deirdre Wilson. 1986 (2nd edition 1995). *Relevance: Communication and Cognition*. Wiley-Blackwell.

Sperber, Dan and Deirdre Wilson. 2015. Beyond speaker meaning. *Croatian Journal of Philosophy* XV.44, pp. 117–149.

Thomas, Jenny. 1983. Cross-cultural pragmatic failure. *Applied Linguistics* 4.2: 91–112.

Wharton, Tim. 2003. Interjections, language and the 'showing/saying' continuum. *Pragmatics and Cognition* 11.1: 39–91.

Wharton, Tim. 2009. *Pragmatics and Nonverbal Communication*. Cambridge University Press.

Wilson, Deirdre and Dan Sperber. 1981. On Grice's theory of conversation. In P. Werth (ed.) *Conversation and Discourse*. Croom Helm: 155–178.

Wray, Alison and Aileen Bloomer. 2012. *Projects in Linguistics and Language Studies*, 3rd edition. Routledge.

Yus, Francisco. 2008. Inferring from comics: a multi-stage account. In Pelegrí Sancho Cremades. Carmen Gregori Signes and Santiago Renard Álvares (eds.) *El Discurs del Comic*. University of Valencia: 223–249.

Zipf, George Kingsley. 1949. *Human Behavior and the Principle of Least Effort*. Addison-Wesley Press.

Yus, Francisco. 2009. Visual metaphor versus verbal metaphor: a unified account. In Charles J. Forceville and Eduardo Urios-Aparisi (eds.) *Multimodal Metaphor*. Mouton de Gruyter: 147–172.

INDEX

Printed in the United States
by Baker & Taylor Publisher Services